S/Sgt. "FROGGY LESUEUR
CHARLIE BAKER
BETTY MEEKS
REV. DAVID MARSHALL LEE
CATHERINE SIMMS
OWEN MUSSER
ELLARD SIMMS

The Place: Betty Meeks' Fishing Lodge Resort, Tilghman
County, Georgia, U.S.A.

The Time: The Recent Past

ACT I

Scene 1: Evening.
Scene 2: The following morning.

ACT II

Scene 1: Afernoon, two days later.
Scene 2: That evening.

D World Lightning

Light check   preshow
              B10
              LQ9

Sound check   preshow
              SQ12
              SQ14

LQ 1 preshow
SQ.5 preshow: 10 mm till GO time
H2H SQ.6 LQ3   - curtain speech   [STOP Sound]
end curtain speech: Hat; LQ5
LQ7 - let establish then cont.
SQ2

THE FOREIGNER

ACT I

SCENE 1

In the darkness, rain and thunder. As the lights come up, we find ourselves in what was once the living-room of a log farm-house, now adapted for service as a parlor for paying guests — middle-income summer people, mostly, who come to fish, and swim, and play a little cards at night, and to fill up on Betty Meeks' away-from-home cooking. We might think it still a living-room were it not for the presence of a small counter with modest candy and tobacco displays, a guest register, and a bell. Also, there is about one sofa too many, a small stove and its woodbin, and a coffee-table, on which a bowl of apples rests. Though we wouldn't know it from the first two dialects we hear, the fact is that we are in Tilghman County, Georgia, U.S.A. — two hours by good road south out of Atlanta, then pull off at Cooley's Food and Bait and call for directions. It used to be that Omer Meeks, who owned the lake house, would then have driven down and led you up the hill in his Dodge pickup. But Omer's gone now, and Betty, his widow, doesn't drive.

Though we won't meet true representatives of either group, the county residents are about equally divided between the very poor — old folks, mostly, who live in hillside dwellings which we might call makeshift before we learned that some of them have been in use for a hundred years — and the very rich, who have bought up most of the lakeside property, erected split-level homes, and put down sod lawns, some of which the owners even mow themselves, enjoying the rough life. Debutantes from the city, recently and happily past virginity, are here, too, with nervous beaux, brought in on the sly while Daddy and Mama are off at the convention. It is spring.

Down the hall somewhere, a door closes, and in, with suitcases, come two Englishmen — damp, but arrived. They are about the same age — late forties, perhaps — but of distinctly different

9

styles. The first, in a British Army fatigue outfit, seems well-fed, flushed with the spirit of adventure, and right at home. The other, standing in his forlorn trenchcoat, seems quietly, somehow permanently, lost. His gaze has come to rest somewhere beyond the wood stove, which lights but does not warm his sad, thin face. He seems almost not to hear his companion, the cheerful patter of whom puts us in mind of those salesmen we have heard in Portobello Road.

FROGGY. 'Ere we go, then, Charlie, 'ere we go. This is the old place, all right. (*Calling out.*) Hullo? Bet? (*Rings the bell.*) Betty, my love? (*To Charlie.*) Wot time d'yer make it? (*Charlie doesn't respond.*) Well, not gone 'alf nine, I shouldn't think. (*Calling.*) Betty! Well—never mind. She can't 'ave gone too far, with the front door wide open like that. Fire in the grate. Unless it's like one o' them ghost ships, eh? (*No response to this hopeful little jest.*) Nah—Betty'll be down directly, and we'll 'ave a nice cuppa somethin' 'ot. That'll be nice, won't it? 'Ere—make ourselves comfortable meanwhile, shall we? Eh? Put another log in that, if yer like. Bit like bed and breakfast, innit? (*Pointing.*) Guest rooms—through there. 'Ot meals cheerfully prepared by the lovely widow Meek's 'erself. Bar. (*Pouring a whiskey.*) One for you, Charlie? I never drink alone. (*No response from Charlie.*) If I can 'elp it. (*Downs his drink.*) 'Ere! Like to see 'ow far we've come tonight? (*Holding up a map.*) Atlanta, there we are. London to Atlanta? Picked up the jeep? 'Undred miles south on the motorway, more or less—turned off round about 'ere, there's the lake, see? (*Starts putting the map away again.*) Oh, it's lovely in daylight, the lake is—see it right from the window. Lovely. Just wot you need, Charlie—your own forest retreat. Silent? Peaceful? Eh? Wot d'yer think?/
CHARLIE. I shouldn't have come.
FROGGY. Now, *now?*
CHARLIE. No, I—oh, don't think me ungrateful, Froggy. I know the enormous trouble you've taken to bring me here—.
FROGGY. No, it was no trouble. Yer know wot I told the Yanks? "'E's my assistant," I says. "If *'e* don't go— *I* don't go." One minute later, bingo. On the plane together. (*A proud chuckle.*)

CHARLIE. Yes—your research assistant—that was a good joke— but—.
FROGGY. It all depends on my approach; the right approach? That's it.
CHARLIE. Yes. . . . Still—.
FROGGY. Wot.
CHARLIE. I should have stayed with Mary, at the hospital. When a man's wife is dying, he belongs with her, not—not in Georgia.
FROGGY. We'll only be 'ere three days.
CHARLIE. Still—with only six months left. Six months. Before she—.
FROGGY. Now, now. Doctors 've been wrong before. Besides which, Mary wanted yer to come 'ere with me, you know that. Fairly begged me to take yer, she did.
CHARLIE. Yes. And so I agreed. But—.
FROGGY. Yes, and she was right, too, if I do say it. The way you were 'angin' about the 'ospital, pinin' away. You were lookin' worse than wot she did.
CHARLIE. Still. . . .
FROGGY. She was worried for yer.
CHARLIE. Hm. . . .
FROGGY. She was. I could see it in 'er eyes.
CHARLIE. (*A great sigh.*) Oh, Froggy.
FROGGY. Wot.
CHARLIE. I don't think worry was what you saw in Mary's eyes.
FROGGY. Wot? 'Course it was.
CHARLIE. Oh, Froggy. For someone I see so little, you're such a good friend, I—. I'm so bad at talking to people. But I—I think you ought to know. Mary—Mary doesn't like me, very much.
FROGGY. Go on. (*"Pull the other."*)
CHARLIE. No, no. The fact is, she finds me boring.
FROGGY. No.
CHARLIE. Yes. Yes. (*Pause.*) Yes. (*Pause.*) That's why she wanted me to go away, you see. She simply finds me shatter-ingly, profoundly—boring.
FROGGY. Now, why would she think that, eh?
CHARLIE. Oh, because I am. I know it. There I've sat behind

11

my grey little proofreader's desk for twenty-seven years, now —. I sometimes wonder whether a science-fiction magazine even *needs* a proofreader. Does anyone really care whether there is one K or two in "Klatu, barada, nikto"? No, no, I'm boring, all right. I've often wondered — how does one acquire personality? What must it be like, to be able to tell a funny story? To arouse laughter. Anger. Respect. To be thought — wise? How must it be?

FROGGY. You were a good officer.

CHARLIE. Not much of a trick in peacetime.

FROGGY. Well, we can't always 'ave wars, yer know. You would've faced enemy fire with the best if you'd 'ad to.

CHARLIE. That is something I shall always wonder.

FROGGY. Well, don't wonder. And don't wonder about Mary, either. I don't know 'er very well, but I know that a looker like wot she is, she's 'ad 'er chances. She could've cast 'er eye on some other bloke, but she never 'as, now, 'as she? (*No answer.*) Eh? (*Pause.*) 'As she?

CHARLIE. (*Who hadn't intended to admit this.*) Oh. . . .

FROGGY. Naaow.

CHARLIE. Yes. . . .

FROGGY. All right, all right. You've caught 'er flirtin' with some bloke, is that it? Caught 'er makin' eyes at some bloke?

CHARLIE. Yes. . . .

FROGGY. Where was it?

CHARLIE. The shower. . . .

FROGGY. Oh, God.

CHARLIE. Yes. . . .

FROGGY. Well, all right, all right. It 'appens in the best of marriages. Eh? One little mistake. One little dalliance, that's no reason for you — for you to —. (*Seeing Charlie's expression.*) More than one? (*Charlie nods.*) More than — two? (*Another nod.*) 'Ow many, then?

CHARLIE. Twenty-three.

FROGGY. Naaow!

CHARLIE. More or less.

FROGGY. Mary?

CHARLIE. Yes. . . .

FROGGY. I don't believe it.

CHARLIE. Quite true. Actors, writers. All the glamorous professions, you see. Criminals. . . . Veterinarians. . . .

FROGGY. Gor . . . ! And did you — know?

CHARLIE. Oh, yes. Mary wanted me to. She flaunted them at me.

FROGGY. Tsk! I don't believe it.

CHARLIE. Well. . . .

FROGGY. And you still — ? I mean, after all that, you still — ?

CHARLIE. Love her? (*Nods.*) More than anything on earth. Love is not love, Froggy, which alters when it alteration finds.

FROGGY. No. . . . (*Pause.*) 'Oo said that?

CHARLIE. Shakespeare.

FROGGY. Ah, yes. (*Pause.*) 'E could turn a phrase, couldn't 'e?

CHARLIE. Yes. . . .

FROGGY. (*Poetically.*) "Love is not love, Froggy, which — " what?

CHARLIE. "Which — which alters when it alteration finds."

FROGGY. Yes. Quite true.

CHARLIE. He — he didn't say "Froggy."

FROGGY. No. No, 'e wouldn't, of course. (*A silence.*) 'Ave you talked to anyone else about this?

CHARLIE. I've tried to. But I — I'm no good at it, you see. Talking. Talk. I — . One is expected to talk these things out, but I — I can't seem to — . I never finish sentences, I — . I have an active fear of — of — of — .

FROGGY. Talk?

CHARLIE. Yes. Lately. Even idle conversation — terrifies me. Simply knowing that in another moment, it's going to be my turn, again. My turn to — to — to — .

FROGGY. To talk.

CHARLIE. Yes.

FROGGY. Well, yer won't 'ave ter worry 'ere. Betty'll do all the talkin' for both of yer.

CHARLIE. (*Alarmed.*) What?

FROGGY. Oh, she's a regular chatterbox, Betty is. Good weather, bad weather, 'ow's yer mum — ?

CHARLIE. Oh, God — .

FROGGY. And when she's not goin' on about somethin', the other guests will be. So don't — .

13

CHARLIE. Other guests?

FROGGY. Well—.

CHARLIE. You mean—*strangers?*

FROGGY. Well, they won't be strangers long. Why, as soon as you've 'ad one or two—.

CHARLIE. Conversations!

FROGGY. Charlie—.

CHARLIE. Take me with you. Please.

FROGGY. I—.

CHARLIE. Please. Try to understand. I *can't*—talk to anyone now. *Please.*

FROGGY. I can't bring a civilian on post, you know that. I—. (*Charlie, in growing panic, holds his chest, grasping for air.*) Charlie? (*Rushing to him.*) Oh, God. 'Ere, look. (*Ready to promise anything.*) All right, yer don't want to 'ave ter talk to anyone? All right, I'll fix it for yer.

CHARLIE. Hm?

FROGGY. I'll fix it. I've brought you 'ere, I'll make it right for yer. If it's no conversation you want, it's no conversation you'll 'ave. Eh? Royal treatment, day and night—baths drawn, meals set out—not a word spoken nor a word required. 'Ow's that?

CHARLIE. But—they'll think me rude.

FROGGY. No, they won't. It all depends on my approach. The right approach, that's it. I can make Betty love the idea, if I put it right. Let's see—. Well, I'll think of somethin', don't worry. (*Taking a key from the wall and giving it to Charlie.*) Ah, number seven, good. 'Ere, you settle in. I'll find Bet, and we'll all 'ave tea in a minute.

CHARLIE. But—she won't speak to me?

FROGGY. I've told yer—nobody in this 'ouse will speak to you for the next three days, or you can dock me to corporal. My word on it! Off! (*Charlie exits.*) Oh, God, wot've I done? Ah, well. (*Betty Meeks enters, arms full of firewood, not seeing Froggy. She is more than seventy, speaks the hardy local dialect, and, like everyone, is wise about some things and naive about others.*) 'Elp yer, Miss?

BETTY. (*Startled.*) Oh! (*Recognizing him—happily.*) Frog! (*They both start hugging and jumping about.*) I'm gettin' ye all wet.

FROGGY. Oh, I've been wet before. You remind me a bit of Malaysia.

BETTY. (*Removing her raincoat.*) Who's she?
FROGGY. No, it's a place. 'Ere, look. (*Retrieving a parcel from his coat pocket.*) I've brought yer something.
BETTY. (*Opening it.*) Spoons!
FROGGY. 'At's right.
BETTY. You know I love spoons.
FROGGY. 'At's right. I know. Bit tricky ter get, some o' these, yer know.
BETTY. Ohh. Now, whar'd ye get this 'un here?
FROGGY. I was given that by one of the aborigines of Canada.
BETTY. My land. Ain't that sump'm.
FROGGY. Yes. And look 'ere—(*Handing her another spoon.*) where d'yer suppose that's from?
BETTY. (*Afraid to guess.*) I don't *know.* . . .
FROGGY. The Mysterious East.
BETTY. (*Reading, in awe.*) "Made in Taiwan."
FROGGY. That's right.
BETTY. My goodness, Frog—the places you been. The people you seen. Jest takes m'breath away. (*With a third spoon.*) And this 'un here, whar's this form?
FROGGY. (*Darkly.*) Tijuana.
BETTY. Ohh. Sounds dangerous.
FROGGY. It is. Yes.
BETTY. Oh, look! I turned it upside down, 'n' all her clothes come off!
FROGGY. Well—they're a heathen people.
BETTY. Land!
FROGGY. Yes.
BETTY. (*Doing as she says.*) Well—this 'un'll have to go in a drawer. But the others I'll leave right out here. There. Ain't they perty?
FROGGY. Not as lovely as you, though.
BETTY. Now.
FROGGY. 'Ow've yer been, then, Bet?
BETTY. Bad. . . .
FROGGY. Naaow.
BETTY. Right bad. I have. Right poorly.
FROGGY. Well, yer look wonderful.
BETTY. Slown' down. Tirin' out. Jest feelin' . . . s'bad.

15

FROGGY. (*His invention failing.*) Well, yer look great.

BETTY. Puny, and sick, an' jest not much interested in things no more. Runnin' down.

FROGGY. No—.

BETTY. Runnin' down. (*Having won.*) How you?

FROGGY. Oh, I'm all right.

BETTY. What ye here doin' this time?

FROGGY. Oh, same job every year, you know. Guest instructor. The American army flies me over. I take out a few o' the young recruits, and tell 'em stories about the bomb squad. Everyone 'as a sandwich and a bit o' fruit. Then we blow up a mountain and 'op it back 'ome. Not bad duty.

BETTY. Ain't that dangerous, though?

FROGGY. *No*, no. Safe as 'ouses. We're miles away when it goes off. Look—. (*He opens what resembles a typewriter case; actually, we see, it is a disassembled manual detonator, complete with plunger, which Froggy quickly assembles.*) My very own design, this. The Froggy LeSueur Portable Detonatin' Device. Light, yet efficient. (*Pointing.*) Positive wire 'ere? (*Pointing.*) Negative? Attach to the load? And—push this down. (*She obeys. He claps.*) One less mountain to worry about. (*Chuckling, he starts taking it apart again.*)

BETTY. (*Having noticed something in the woodbin.*) Well, would you look at this.

FROGGY. Wot?

BETTY. Two of 'em, this time. That boy.

FROGGY. Eh?

BETTY. It's that dumb little Ellard Simms, looky here. He takes one o' my apples, bites out of it, then decides he don't want it, and dumps it in here.

FROGGY. Oh, yes.

BETTY. Ever' day. He does it ever' day. An' scoldin' him don't do no good, 'cause he's jest a little half-wit, ye know. But that's a waste, ain't it? Good winesap apples, too. (*She tosses them away and begins putting wood into the stove.*) Reverend David says I jest oughta fergive 'im, but then he's about the sweet-temperedest man they is on this earth.

FROGGY. Reverend David?

BETTY. No, you don't know David, do ye? Nor Miz Catherine, neither, *do* ye? Lordy, the things that's gone on here lately.

Y'see—Ellard's Catherine's baby brother, and Catherine and David's engaged. They're stayin' here now.

FROGGY. Ah.

BETTY. Separate rooms.

FROGGY. Of course.

BETTY. An' after they're married—they might buy the house.

FROGGY. The—? *This* 'ouse?

BETTY. (*Not looking at him.*) Well, yes, they—might.

FROGGY. Bet!

BETTY. I know. It's even hard fer me t' say it, sometimes.

FROGGY. But—you've always 'ad this 'ouse. I thought—.

BETTY. Oh, Frog. It's been awful bad lately. There 'uz a lot a' damage here over the winter. Spent my last nickel fixin' that, 'n' now it looks like none o' the reg'lar summer folks is comin' at *all*, so—.

FROGGY. Why not?

BETTY. Oh, they're scairt it ain't safe here no more.

FROGGY. Not safe?

BETTY. No, it 'uz that Owen Musser started that talk. Mean ol' thing. He got himself made property inspector fer Tilghman County, an' now he's sayin' my foundations is rotten, an' I'm liable to get condemned. You see that pile o' new bricks?

FROGGY. In the car park, yeh.

BETTY. Yeah, I went 'n' bought 'em. Gettin' bricklayers at twenty dollars an hour, though—I cain't afford that. Not 'less we get some business in here.

FROGGY. Property's a bit cheaper if it's condemned, I suppose?

BETTY. Oh, yes. Yes, sir—Owen gets this place condemned, I cain't even sell the house, jest the land under it. That's the law.

FROGGY. 'E 'asn't got an interest in the place, 'as 'e?

BETTY. Owen? Noo. Owen couldn't even afford that little bush out there.

FROGGY. Then these young people 'ave got money, 'ave they?

BETTY. Well, Catherine does, yes. Catherine's daddy was Simms Prepared Meats, which I reckon you heared of.

FROGGY. I might 'a' done.

BETTY. So, yes, she's real well off. She's the whole family now. Her 'n' Ellard.

FROGGY. Well, *Bet*—if yer sell, where will yer live?

17

BETTY. Oh, I don't know. It won't matter. If I have to move out of this old place, I don't s'pose it'll be too long till Meeks 'n' me is together again.

FROGGY. Get off.

BETTY. No, I tell ye, Frog. Lately, I been — addin' things up.

FROGGY. Bet!

BETTY. No, I have. And I tell ye — the one thing — the only thing I regret — and don't tell nobody this — .

FROGGY. No.

BETTY. — was I wisht I'd managed to see some o' the world, sometime. The way you done. Is it sinful of me to wish that, you reckon?

FROGGY. No.

BETTY. Afore you come along, I never even knowed nobody from outside Tilghman. Then hearin' all your tales about them A-rabs, 'n' Greekses, 'n' such-like? Laws. I lay awake sometimes, wonderin' what them folks 'd be like. Foreigners. Their different kinds a' lives? How they dress up, 'n' talk, 'n' all? Well. Too late now. Y' get old afore y' get around t' some things.

FROGGY. Well, yer might be disappointed, anyway.

BETTY. Well, I wonder.

FROGGY. Oh, yeh, love, take my word on it. Your typical foreigner? No, you 'aven't missed much. No. Bit on the dull side, really. Bit borin'. Quite borin', in fact. Dresses about like wot we do. And of course, it's useless to say anything to 'im, because 'e doesn't — . 'E doesn't speak — . 'Old on.

BETTY. What's wrong? (*Froggy clears his throat.*) Well, what's the matter, Frog?

FROGGY. Me? Nothin'. Look 'ere, Bet — .

BETTY. Yes?

FROGGY. Ah — .

BETTY. What is it?

FROGGY. Just thinkin'. . . .

BETTY. *What.*

FROGGY. Right . . . right. Look, Bet, I've somethin' to tell yer. There's this bloke, he's a mate of mine, I've brought along.

BETTY. Here?

FROGGY. That's right. 'E's in my old room now. 'E'll be stoppin' 'ere for three days. I want yer to take super care of 'im — best of everything, right?

18

BETTY. Well, yes?

FROGGY. All right. The other thing is — oh, God, 'ow should I put this? 'E mustn't be spoken to.

BETTY. He mustn't — when?

FROGGY. Ever.

BETTY. Mustn't be spoken to?

FROGGY. No.

BETTY. Why not?

FROGGY. Well — .

BETTY. Somethin' wrong with him?

FROGGY. No. No. Perfectly nice. Terrific fella. But — the fact is — 'e doesn't speak English very well.

BETTY. No?

FROGGY. No. In fact — not a word.

BETTY. Oh?

FROGGY. No, poor bloke. Now, I can't say too much, mind. I've got my orders. But I'll tell yer this — if someone 'ere was wishin' ter see a foreigner — a real one — p'raps they wouldn't 'ave ter look too far.

BETTY. Frog!

FROGGY. That's right.

BETTY. You mean this fella you brought with ye — is — ?

FROGGY. As foreign as the day is long.

BETTY. Where's he from?

FROGGY. Where?

BETTY. What country?

FROGGY. Uh — no. I'm sorry. I can't say more. My tongue is tied.

BETTY. Oh! Is he — you don't mean he's here on some kinda special government work?

FROGGY. I won't say yes, and I won't say no.

BETTY. Well, my land. What's his name?

FROGGY. Charlie.

BETTY. Charlie?

FROGGY. Yeh, Well — I mean, his real name is Cha-Oo-Lee, or somethin' like that. But I calls 'im Charlie.

BETTY. (*A sudden thought. Lowering her voice.*) He ain't — he ain't a *Communist*, is he?

FROGGY. Wot, 'im? Naaow. Naaow — 'e's got a stack o' credit cards in 'is wallet that thick.

BETTY. Oh, good.

FROGGY. Yes.

BETTY. But — we cain't none of us talk to him?

FROGGY. No, it shames 'im, yer see. Poor bloke — 'e can't reply to wot people say, and then 'e feels 'orrible. If yer so much as says, "Good mornin'" to 'im, 'e walks about, 'angin' is 'ead for days. Yer don't want that.

BETTY. Why, no. Poor man.

FROGGY. 'E'll be no trouble. Regular meals, spot o' tea once in a while.

BETTY. My. A real foreigner.

FROGGY. Don't expect Jojo the Jungle Boy. 'E's just a bloke, yer know.

BETTY. Still — .

FROGGY. You'll get on great. I wish I could stay, but I'm off. I, uh — (*Smiling.*) I suppose I ought to 'ave just a word with Cha-Oo-Lee.

BETTY. You know how to speak his kinda talk?

FROGGY. Well, the odd phrase. You know — "'Ello" — "Where's the gents'?" — "My hat is brown," that sort o' thing.

BETTY. Oh — .(*Perhaps she is about to ask for a quick language course, but she is interrupted by a sound from the hall.*)

FROGGY. That'll be 'im. Eh — could you — get 'im some tea, dear?

BETTY. Oh, surely, (*Exiting to the kitchen.*) Laws, laws. (*Charlie enters, and goes listlessly to a chair.*)

FROGGY. Eh — Charlie — .

CHARLIE. Not now, Froggy. Let me just sit here for a little.

FROGGY. Well — . (*Too late. Betty enters with a teacup, sees Charlie, who is seated facing away from her. She pantomines to Froggy: "Is this Charlie?" Froggy nods. Betty, her lips pressed excitedly together, goes to Charlie and silently presents him with tea. Charlie looks at her.*)

CHARLIE. Thank you. (*Betty, surprised, looks at Froggy, who shrugs. Then she looks back at Charlie, with an excited smile.*)

BETTY. (*As if encouraging a partly-deaf child.*) That was *real good!* (*Charlie stares at her.*)

FROGGY. Uh, Charlie — . (*Charlie looks at him.*) Uh — (*Going to him.*) gomo rum diddly-moo a second, will yer? (*Charlie stares. Are all the people mad? Froggy turns to Betty, smiles.*) If yer could excuse us for a moment, pet.

BETTY. Why, certainly. (*Exiting.*) Laws, laws. — warn David!

CHARLIE. What on earth—?

FROGGY. Sh! Now, Charlie, just listen. I've fixed it for yer. Yer won't be bothered from now on.

CHARLIE. Why? What have you done?

FROGGY. I've told 'er yer can't speak English.

CHARLIE. What?

FROGGY. Look—.

CHARLIE. You've told her I can't—?

FROGGY. Speak English.

CHARLIE. Why?

FROGGY. Look. Remember wot you said? "I don't want ter seem rude." Well—this way, yer won't be. You're waited on 'and and foot, not a word spoken, right? Lovely. Wot do you have to do? Nothin'. Wot do you have to say? Nothin'. Are they offended? No. They *love* yer for it.

CHARLIE. But—.

FROGGY. Betty, you saw Betty. She *already* loves yer. Why, you're picturesque.

CHARLIE. Froggy, no.

FROGGY. Why not?

CHARLIE. I can't.

FROGGY. Can't wot?

CHARLIE. Pretend.

FROGGY. (*Trying not to shout.*) Yer don't 'ave ter *do* anything! Yer *sit* there. Yer bring a bit o' glamour to a sweet old lady's twilight years, and yer bring yerself a bit o' quiet, eh? You said yer can't talk to anyone.

CHARLIE. No, I—I can. I was panicking. I—.

FROGGY. Yer *can.*

CHARLIE. Yes.

FROGGY. Well, that's all right, then. You be the one to tell 'er.

CHARLIE. Tell her what?

FROGGY. (*Putting on coat.*) Why, that we've lied to 'er. That we've raised, 'er 'opes, only ter dash 'em to the ground again.

CHARLIE. *We?*

FROGGY. Yes, well—I'll be glad I'm gone. I won't 'ave ter see 'er disappointed little eyes fill with tears, and watch 'er hackin' at

21

'er little wrists with a meat-knife. (*Going.*) Ta-ta.

CHARLIE. (*Stopping him.*) Frog.

FROGGY. (*Turning back at the entranceway.*) Eh?

CHARLIE. (*With a smile that asks forgiveness.*) I can't do it. I'm sorry. I simply can't.

FROGGY. (*Giving in.*) No. Suppose not. Daft idea, really. Well—when Betty comes in, tell her I was just jokin', then, all right? She'll understand, don't worry.

CHARLIE. All right.

FROGGY. You be all right?

CHARLIE. Yes. Thanks.

FROGGY. Good. So long.

CHARLIE. So long. (*A door slams.*)

FROGGY. 'Ello, 'Oo's this?

DAVID. (*Entering, in a wet poncho.*) Whoo! (*Sees Froggy.*) Hello. (*He starts pulling off his poncho, stamping.*)

FROGGY. 'Ello.

DAVID. Man, that is what we call a frogstrangler, out there. That is a *storm.* (*The poncho has come off, to reveal a friendly, open face. David, we see, is neither the stereotypically pallid, remote young divinity student, nor the hearty, backslapping evangelist. He seems rather to be a regular fella—humorous, and open, and, it would appear, a good young man to have on our side.*) You're not planning to go out *in* that, are you?

FROGGY. Oh, I'm not worried.

DAVID. All right. No, I wasn't worried either, till I saw that old fella gatherin' up those animals two by two, and puttin' 'em on that boat. Then—. (*Froggy laughs.*) I don't know. (*Noticing the uniform.*) Are you—? You must be Froggy LeSueur.

FROGGY. That's right.

DAVID. Betty's good friend, *well*—(*Extending his hand.*) I'm David. David Lee.

FROGGY. Lee? As in Robert E.?

DAVID. Yes, sir.

FROGGY. Any relation?

DAVID. Distant.

FROGGY. 'E was a great strategist.

DAVID. I know that.

FROGGY. Oh! *Re*verend David.

DAVID. Yes.

FROGGY. Betty says yer might buy the place.

DAVID. Well, we do love this old lodge. Of course, what we really hope is that Betty won't end up having to sell. But—.

FROGGY. Yes, well—you'd do right by 'er, I know.

DAVID. Oh, yes. I don't think we would argue with—whatever price Betty thought was fair.

FROGGY. That's good. Well—give 'er my best. Ta-ta.

DAVID. Good to meet you, sir.

FROGGY. Don't call me sir. I ain't no bloody officer. (*David laughs. Froggy is gone. David turns back to find, in the other entryway, the formidable little figure of Catherine Simms. Her crossed arms, and the basilisk glare from her pretty face, tell us that David has stayed too long at the fair.*)

DAVID. Hi, honey! (*No answer—only that look.*) Honey? What's wrong? (*Charlie, thinking perhaps to excuse himself, starts to get up.*)

CATHERINE. I'm pregnant. (*Charlie freezes in mid-rise.*) You're not so sterile after all. Idn' that good news, Honey? (*Charlie quickly sits again, trying his best to look like a doily.*)

DAVID. (*After a long silence.*) Oh.

CATHERINE. (*With an exasperated sigh, looking away from him.*) Yeah.

DAVID. Oh, well, honey—if you really are—. (*She turns away as he goes to her.*) Now, come here, now—.

CATHERINE. No.

DAVID. Come here. (*She allows herself to be held.*) If you really are—what then, do you think?

CATHERINE. I don't know. Then I guess I go up to Atlanta, and find somebody who can—.

DAVID. Honey. No.

CATHERINE. What do you mean, no?

DAVID. Honey, don't even—.

CATHERINE. This is me we're talkin' about. You think I'm gonna walk down that aisle all ballooned up as big as a house in front of all my people? No, sir. No, I am not. Noo.

DAVID. Honey, no. Listen—we'll get married right away, then. We don't have to wait till November. We'll do it now.

CATHERINE. I don't want to do it now! It's planned for November. Oh, David. How did this happen?

DAVID. It's a miracle, that's what it is. That's what I think it is. Can't you see it that way? I think it must've been supposed to happen.

CATHERINE. Yeah, well, I didn't suppose it to happen. You didn't suppose it to happen. You told me you could never have any—.

DAVID. I know.

CATHERINE. So who supposed it to happen? The good Lord, I suppose?

DAVID. I think so. Yes.

CATHERINE. Yeah, well, that's fine for Him. He's not the one that's gonna have to—. (*She stops short of complete blasphemy.*)

DAVID. Oh, honey, I know how you feel.

CATHERINE. No, you don't.

DAVID. Yes, I do. You feel trapped, and wronged, and not— ready, and I don't blame you. But, honey—I love you. And now it looks like we're meant to have a family. I say let's celebrate. I say let's just do it. (*A long pause.*)

CATHERINE. You really want to?

DAVID. Yes. (*They are embracing now — Catherine facing Charlie's chair.*)

CATHERINE. Can I ask you something?

DAVID. Anything you want.

CATHERINE. (*See Charlie.*) Who the hell are *you*?

DAVID. What?

CATHERINE. (*Turning David around.*) Look!

DAVID. Oh!

CATHERINE. I mean, would you look at that? Would you take a look at the nerve of that? (*To Charlie.*) You were just sittin' there this whole *time*?

DAVID. Now, honey, I'm sure—.

CATHERINE. I don't be*lieve* it!

BETTY. (*Entering.*) What's goin' on in here?

CATHERINE. I can't get over it! We're in here havin' this *real* personal conversation. Then we turn around, what do we see? This *man* sittin' here. Just sittin' here listenin' to every word we *said*.

BETTY. Miz Catherine—.

CATHERINE. I can't get over it! I never heard of anything so *rude*! When I think what we were talkin' about, I—.

24

BETTY. Miz—.

CATHERINE. I could just *die!*

BETTY. He didn't hear ye, Miz Catherine.

CATHERINE. He was sittin' right here the whole—.

BETTY. *Shh,* now? He don't speak no English.

CATHERINE. What?

BETTY. No. Nary a word. So you can just simmer down.

CATHERINE. He doesn't speak English?

BETTY. No. Well, he can say, "Thank you," but he jest learned that tonight.

CATHERINE. Who is he?

BETTY. He's a foreign fella, name's Charlie. (*To Charlie, patting him on the shoulder and shouting in his face.*) *Don't you worry none, Charlie! Everything's gonna be fine!* (*For Charlie, it is surely the moment of truth. If he is to speak, it had better be now. He opens his mouth.*)

CATHERINE. I'd die if I thought he'd been listenin' to us. I would just die. (*Charlie closes his mouth, then opens it to speak again.*)

DAVID. Honey, he wasn't. No decent person would've just sat there. (*Again, Charlie wavers.*)

BETTY. 'Course not. An' Frog wouldn't lie to me. He's m' friend. (*Charlie looks miserably from face to face—Catherine's suspicious, David's trusting, and Betty's shining with pride. Finally, resignedly—perhaps even with an attempt at foreign dialect—he speaks and seals his fate.*)

CHARLIE. Thank you.

BETTY. There, y' see? "Thank you." That's all he knows.

CATHERINE. All right, then.

DAVID. All right. (*To Catherine.*) You all right?

CATHERINE. Where's he from? What's he doin here?

BETTY. I cain't tell ye too much. I got my orders. But Frog says none of us should talk to 'im 'cause it makes him ashamed. *Ain't that right, Charlie?*

DAVID. Well, Bet. *You're* talkin' to him.

BETTY. He likes me to talk to 'im. I was the one that first got him to say, "Thank you." *Wudn' I, Charlie!* (*Charlie smiles wanly.*) See how his face lights up?

CATHERINE. He looks kinda sick to me.

BETTY. He does not.

CATHERINE. I think he does. (*Charlie tries to do a little bow and leave.*)

25

BETTY. No, now. (*To Catherine.*) I think he knows we're talkin' about him. (*Seating him again.*) *Jest set down again, Charlie!* (*Pointing with an enormous, repeated arc into Charlie's teacup.*) *I'll get ye some more nice tea!* (*Charlie moves to object.*) *No, now! It ain't no trouble at all!* (*She starts out again, then sees one of the bitten apples, stops, and holds it out toward Catherine.*) Here, look'ye.

CATHERINE. Oh, no.

BETTY. Yeah. They 'uz two more of 'em in the woodbin this time.

CATHERINE. Oh, Ellard.

BETTY. I tell ye, if that boy was mine — .

CATHERINE. Yeah, well, he's not. He's not mine, either. If I get after him about somethin', he just claims not to remember it. What am I supposed to do, lock him in his room?

DAVID. Honey, now, maybe he doesn't remember doing these things.

CATHERINE. Oh, he does, too — .

DAVID. No, we don't know that. Maybe these things he does are just — subconscious calls for help. Or attention.

CATHERINE. May be. I swear, he's never done so many screwy things before in his life.

DAVID. Well — .

CATHERINE. Then pretended he hadn't.

DAVID. Let me talk to Ellard again. It might be just a phase.

CATHERINE. It better be.

DAVID. It is, I hope it is. I hope he's not — .

CATHERINE. What.

DAVID. Well, I was going to say — getting worse.

CATHERINE. Oh, Lord. Worse.

DAVID. Well, it's nothing to worry about tonight, anyhow.

BETTY. Well — you're a good man. You make me ashamed, sometimes.

DAVID. No, now. You go on and — .

BETTY. (*Starting out again.*) Owen! (*She has found herself suddenly in the dank presence of Owen Musser. Psychologists tell us to beware of a man with two tattoos. One, he may have gotten on a drunk or a dare. But two means he went back. Owen is a two-tatto man.*)

OWEN. (*With a smile we can almost smell.*) Hey, Bet. Nice weather fer eels.

BETTY. Owen, what're you doin' in here?

26

OWEN. It 'uz rainin' outside.

BETTY. You come to see me?

OWEN. No'm. (*Pointing to David.*) Come to see him.

BETTY. 'Bout what?

OWEN. Things.

BETTY. You come up here to spread more gossip about this house?

OWEN. Gossip? (*He smiles, goes to the bar for a Coke.*) No, ma'am—y' see, I'm the Tilghman County property inspector now. Whatever I say, I might say sump'm about you, or your family, or your guests, or your dog, and ye could maybe call that gossip. But I say sump'm about this lodge—now, that ain't gossip. That's the law.

BETTY. (*Going out.*) The law. Anybody'd think you'd been made sheriff.

OWEN. (*Looking at David.*) Don't you laugh. Someday I might be. (*To Betty.*) What would you think of that?

BETTY. You want some ice fer that?

OWEN. No'm. I like it hot.

BETTY. All right. (*Exits into kitchen. Thunder and lightning. Owen shivers.*)

OWEN. I ain't goin' out thar while it's like this. You couldn't *get* me to go. They's things out thar, nights like this, an' that's true. The lightnin' brings 'em out. They'uz a man melted out thar in them hills oncet. They found him right after one, o' these storms, too. Nobody knowed what happened, but he wuz jest melted down like talla'—'cep' fer 'is teeth, 'n' his bones, 'n' the zipper on 'is britches. Now, that's true. They's things out thar.

DAVID. Did you want to talk to me, Owen?

OWEN. In private, I do.

CATHERINE. Well. (*With a wry look at David.*) I'll tear myself away.

DAVID. I'll be up to say goodnight.

CATHERINE. Don't be too long.

DAVID. Don't worry.

CATHERINE. And could you bring me a candle?

DAVID. A candle?

CATHERINE. Yeah, another candle. Mine's about shot.

DAVID. I'll get you one. Sure.

CATHERINE. 'Night.

27

OWEN. 'Night.

DAVID. G'night, honey. (*She is out.*)

OWEN. She go through a lot o' candles, does she? (*David looks at him. Betty re-enters with Charlie's tea.*) Whatcha got thar?

BETTY. Tea. You want some?

OWEN. No'm. (*To David.*) Is they someplace we can talk?

BETTY. You gonna talk, you'll do it right here. No visitors upstairs, that's the rules. (*Gives Charlie his tea.*) An' don't you go drivin' Charlie off, neither.

DAVID. We won't bother him. (*Owen looks at Charlie.*)

BETTY. Goodnight, then. Lock up, will ye, David?

DAVID. I will. Thanks.

BETTY. Don't believe ever'thing ye hear.

DAVID. Don't worry, Betty.

BETTY. 'Night, Owen.

OWEN. (*Still watching Charlie.*) 'Night.

BETTY. 'Night, Charlie! (*She leaves. Owen is still scrutinizing Charlie, who watches him back coolly.*)

DAVID. (*Looking at Charlie, smiling.*) Go ahead, don't worry about Charlie.

OWEN. What is he? Deef?

DAVID. No, he's not deaf. He doesn't speak English.

OWEN. He—?

DAVID. That's right.

OWEN. What's he doin' *here*?

DAVID. I don't know, Owen. A friend of Betty's brought him over.

OWEN. He don't understand me, huh?

DAVID. No.

OWEN. Nary a word?

DAVID. Nope.

OWEN. Well. . . . (*Looking at Charlie and smiling.*) 'Zat right? A foreigner, huh? Huh, Charlie? (*Shakes his head, with a warm chuckle.*) Well—we don't get s' many o' your kind in these parts. (*Rubs his chin.*) Why—last time I saw a foreigner, he was wrigglin' on the end o' my bayonet. (*Charlie watches him evenly, smiling a little. Owen is smiling too.*) Hey, dummy? (*To David.*) He really don't know what I'm sayin', huh?

DAVID. No.

OWEN. No, reckon not. 'Cause if he did, I'd know it. I would.

I'm smart about some things. Like when people's playactin' on me? (*Circling behind Charlie's chair.*) I always can catch 'em. I catch 'em ever' time. An' then, ye know what I do? I pour hot Coke down their necks, like this—. (*Charlie, now looking toward David, remains blandly beatific. Owen, of course, does not pour Coke down Charlie's neck.*) Well. This is sorta fun. Say anything you want to him, long 's you're smilin', cain't ye? (*In front of Charlie again.*) Hey, Charlie? Whar's your mother? Huh? Where's she at now? Down under ground, someplace? Some foreign grave-yard the hell off someplace, pushin' up—palm trees, 'er sump'm? Wonder what she looks like now. You ever wonder that? What she looks like right now? They's probably not enough of 'er left to spread on toast. (*A wide smile.*) Whaddaya say to that? Huh? Ain't you got nothin' to say to that? Huh?

CHARLIE. (*With great calm.*) Thank you.

OWEN. (*Laughing.*) *Yee*-hee! Y' hear that? "Thank you!" Don't that jest beat it? "Thank you," he says!

DAVID. That's all he knows.

OWEN. Well, that's real good, Charlie. You're gonna be some fun to have around. Yes sir. I am gonna have some fun with you.

DAVID. I've got to get upstairs, Owen.

OWEN. You do, huh?

DAVID. I've had a long day.

• OWEN. You talk any sense into them Atlanta boys?

DAVID. Not yet. But I think they'll come around.

OWEN. Well—I got some news. I got me back a little piece a' paper today. You wanta see?

DAVID. What is it? (*Owen hands him a paper, which he unfolds.*) "Condemned."

OWEN. 'At's right. Certified by the state office. This place jest turned into a real bargain.

DAVID. Interesting.

OWEN. I thought ye might think so.

DAVID. So how much can Betty ask for it now?

OWEN. Tops, around twenty thousand.

DAVID. That is a bargain, truly.

OWEN. You gonna buy it, then?

DAVID. As soon as I'm able.

OWEN. You be careful she don't find herself another buyer.

DAVID. No, Betty will wait till I have the funds.

OWEN. She gonna wait six months?

DAVID. If need be.

OWEN. (*With paper.*) 'Cause this ain't necessarily permanent, ye know. That there brickwork out front gets repaired, 'n' you got yerself one expensive little property again.

DAVID. Just the brickwork, huh?

OWEN. Thass' all. She fixes that up, an' they ain't nothin' I can do. Legally.

DAVID. Uh-huh. Well—I don't think we have to—. (*He stops, seeing Ellard in the hall entrance. David smiles.*) Well, hey, Ellard. How're you doing? (*There doesn't, we must admit, seem to be much to Ellard. He is a lumpy, overgrown, backward youth, who spends much of his time kneading something tiny and invisible in front of his chest.*) You know Owen? Owen Musser?

OWEN. Hey.

DAVID. What you been up to?

ELLARD. Where's Cath at?

DAVID. She went on upstairs.

ELLARD. Okay—. (*Starts off.*)

DAVID. I tell you—you could do me a favor, Ellard. You want to do me a favor?

ELLARD. Yeah.

DAVID. All right. Go in the kitchen, in the refrigerator, get a carrot. And take it up to Catherine, will you?

ELLARD. A *carrot.*

DAVID. Yeah, a carrot. You know what a carrot is.

ELLARD. Yeah, I know.

DAVID. Of course you do. Could you do that for me, then?

ELLARD. Get her a carrot?

DAVID. Yes. She wanted one. I said I'd bring it up, but I can't get away right now.

ELLARD. All right. . . .

DAVID. That'd be a big favor, thank you. (*Ellard exits into the kitchen.*) Ellard. Poor boy.

OWEN. What's the matter with 'im?

DAVID. Oh, no one knows. He just needs a lot of patience. And he's worse just lately. Their daddy dying and all, I guess is what it is. Sad thing.

OWEN. He ain't gettin' none of their daddy's money, is he?

DAVID. Ellard? No. Not likely.

OWEN. (*Turning on him.*) You mean he *might?*

DAVID. Oh—theoretically, he's supposed to receive half of the family money.

OWEN. What?

DAVID. *But*, only if Catherine should decide he's intelligent enough.

OWEN. If he's intelligent enough?

DAVID. That's right.

OWEN. Well, that don't seem too likely, does it?

DAVID. No.

OWEN. (*Looking at Charlie.*) House is *full* of dummies, ain't it? (*Ellard re-enters with a carrot.*)

DAVID. That's good. You have any trouble?

ELLARD. No.

DAVID. That's fine. Could you take it up, then? I'll be up in a minute, tell her.

ELLARD. All right. . . .

DAVID. Thank you, Ellard. (*Ellard exits.*)

OWEN. Intelligent enough, huh? (*Snorts.*) Hunnerd thousand dollars, er so? He'd probably spend it on bubble gum, er sump'm.

DAVID. I really must go up, Owen. Thanks for your news. I'll take it from here.

OWEN. (*Making sure.*) You *will.*

DAVID. I will.

OWEN. You better.

DAVID. Just have faith, Owen. The Lord will provide. If He wishes Tilghman County to have a good Christian hunt club, then Tilghman County shall have one.

CATHERINE. (*Off.*) David!

OWEN. 'Night.

DAVID. 'Night, Owen. Be careful. (*Owen goes.*)

CATHERINE. (*Off.*) David!

DAVID. I'm just locking up, honey.

CATHERINE. (*Entering, with Ellard trailing sheepishly behind.*) David, you know anything about this?

DAVID. What?

CATHERINE. *What* is this?

DAVID. Well—uh, that's a carrot.

CATHERINE. I *know* it's a carrot.

DAVID. Yeah?

31

CATHERINE. Did you tell Ellard to bring me a carrot?

DAVID. No, I told him to bring you a candle.

CATHERINE. Oh, Ellard.

ELLARD. He said a carrot.

DAVID. It doesn't matter, honey.

CATHERINE. Ellard, he didn't say "carrot." He said "candle."

DAVID. No, it's all right babe. He was trying to do me a favor. Here, here's a candle.

ELLARD. He said bring you a carrot.

CATHERINE. Ellard, damn it, he did not.

DAVID. Honey. Maybe I did.

CATHERINE. Oh—!

DAVID. I might have. I was talking with Owen, maybe I turned around and said "carrot" by mistake.

CATHERINE. Oh, David, you did not. Nobody says "carrot" instead of "candle."

DAVID. Honey, it doesn't matter. Come here. (*They embrace.*)

CATHERINE. Lord. What a day.

DAVID. I know. How you doin'? You all right, now?

CATHERINE. I guess.

DAVID. All right. Go on up, then, I'll be there directly.

CATHERINE. All right. Come on, Ellard.

ELLARD. (*As they leave.*) I thought he said carrot.

CATHERINE. I don't want to hear any more about it, Ellard. (*David watches them until they leave. Then he picks up an apple from the bowl on the table, polishing it on his chest. He turns to Charlie, smiles.*)

DAVID. There's a good first lesson for you, Charlie—. (*David takes a bite from the apple, chews it thoughtfully, and drops the apple into the woodbin.*) God helps those—who help themselves. (*And he is gone. Charlie stands, watching after him.*)

BLACKOUT

ACT I

SCENE 2

The following morning. Bright sunlight. Betty enters, pulls up a throw-rug in the middle of the floor, and stamps a couple of times.

32

BETTY. Ellard! You down thar yet? Ellard! (*Stamps again.*)
They's only one ladder, ye cain't miss it. Ellard!
CATHERINE. (*Entering, apparently after a rough night.*) What's
goin' on? What time is it?
BETTY. Oh, I 'uz hopin' Ellard could hand me up some
sauerkraut from the cellar. Ellard! Don't reckon he got lost,
do ye?
CATHERINE. How many rooms down there?
BETTY. One.
CATHERINE. Yeah. Probably lost (*She exits.*)
BETTY. (*Going out again.*) Well—do it myself, I reckon.
(*Charlie enters in his robe, looks about, then hurriedly dials the phone.*)
CHARLIE. Oh, *do* hurry . . . Hello? May I speak with Staff
Sergeant LeSueur, please? Charlie Baker. No, it's not a code,
it's my name. . . . Hello, Froggy? Could you come get me,
please? Froggy, you don't know what you've done. No, I mean
my pretending not to speak English. . . . No, well, I decided to,
after all. Oh, I overheard something I shouldn't have,
and—well, it seemed best. But Froggy—they don't leave me
alone. No! The old woman does nothing but shout at me. The
others talk about me as if I were a potted palm. That screaming
girl, and her poor addled brother? One thoroughly unpleasant
chap began saying the most awful things about my mother. . . .
Well, something to the effect that he doubted there were enough
of her left to spread on toast. I don't know. No, of course I
sha'n't tell Mother, but still—. And that minister, something
very odd going on with him, I think. I don't know. What is a
"Christian hunt club"? No. Nor I. Yes, I'll hold on. (*Ellard
enters, and stands looking at Charlie. Charlie smiles back at him.*)
ELLARD. Where's Betty at?
CHARLIE. Thank you. (*Ellard heaves a great, confused sigh, and
exits. Into phone.*) No. That was the boy. I don't think he knows
about me yet. Yes, he is rather hopeless, I'm afraid; still, I can't
help feeling that he's being—. (*Betty is entering.*) Zhmeetko az-
mad yi—uh, Gallipoli, m'nyeh.
BETTY. Well! *Good mornin', Charlie!* You must be talkin' to
Frog. *Hey*, Frog! (*Charlie hands her the phone.*) I want to tell
ye—Charlie is the sweetest thing in the whole wide world! Yes!
Now, what does he like fer breakfast? All righty! No, no trouble. No! I swar, he makes me feel twenty years younger. About

33

thirteen. Yeah! You done saved my life when you brung him here. Well—here he is back. (*She hands Charlie the phone, they exchange smiles, then she stamps in the middle of the floor again.*) Ellard! You down thar yet! That boy—. (*To Charlie.*) Go on with yer talk.

CHARLIE. (*Into phone.*) Peevno . . . omsk—uh—.

BETTY. (*Tickled to death.*) Laws, laws. (*She is gone. Charlie watches after her, his escape plan in tatters.*)

CHARLIE. Frog? Yes. Sorry. No, never mind. Don't send the jeep. No. No—it's only two days. But I want to say this, Froggy. And it's important—. (*Betty re-enters. Charlie gives up. Into phone.*) Peem? Bosco-bosco. (*He hangs up.*)

BETTY. Ellard? You down thar now?

ELLARD. (*Faintly, from below.*) Yes'm.

BETTY. You on the ladder? (*No answer.*) Are you on the ladder, Ellard?

ELLARD. I don't know.

BETTY. What?

ELLARD. It's too dark.

BETTY. Would ye jest reach up an' see 'f ye can feel that cross-bar? Ye feel that?

ELLARD. I think so.

BETTY. Now slide it over 'n' open up the door. But remember, watch out the door don't drop down an' hit ye on—.

ELLARD. Ow!

BETTY. On the head. (*The trap door has, of course, opened downward into the floor.*) You all right?

ELLARD. (*To whom this is nothing new.*) Yeah.

BETTY. All right. Hand me that sauerkraut. (*A hand filled with sauerkraut comes out of the floor.*) Ellard—whar's the jar I gave ye? (*Another hand, holding an empty jar, emerges from the floor.*) Oh, Ellard.

ELLARD. *Aah!* (*Both hands disappear quickly, and we hear a thud far below.*)

BETTY. Ellard, are you all right?

ELLARD. Yes'm!

BETTY. Here. Do this instead. Close this door. Slide the bar across. Then go to the barrel, fill up the jar with sauerkraut, and bring it with ye when ye come up.

ELLARD. All right.

34

BETTY. That boy. I tell ye. (*The trap door bangs.*)

ELLARD. Ow!

BETTY. Ellard—come up the way ye went down—through the back door! (*She starts out. Catherine enters.*)

CATHERINE. Have you seen David?

BETTY. No'm, not this mornin'. (*She goes into the kitchen.*)

CATHERINE. Can you see his car out there?

BETTY. (*Off.*) No ma'am, it's gone.

CATHERINE. Shoot! I can't believe that! Without so much as a word *again*. (*To Charlie.*) I told him last night, I'm supposed to be—. Oh, hell. What 'm I talkin' to you for? I'm just goin' nuts, I guess. Nobody to talk to, I'm probably just ready for the funny farm. Shoot. *Shoot.*

BETTY. (*Off.*) Thank ye, Ellard.

CATHERINE. Ellard! Did you see David?

ELLARD. (*Entering.*) Naw. He wud'n' in the basement.

CATHERINE. I didn't suppose he was in the basement. Off with the damn poor people again, is where he is. Helpin' 'em skin hogs, and make soap, and lookin' after their damn souls. I just hope he won't mind havin' a wife he has to go visit in the *insane asylum*!

BETTY. (*Entering.*) What would ye like fer breakfast?

CATHERINE. I don't want any breakfast.

BETTY. Now, Catherine.

CATHERINE. I *don't*. Now? Don't ask me again. I don't.

BETTY. All right. Ellard?

ELLARD. Huh?

BETTY. I'm makin' Charlie some eggs, but I know you don't like eggs. So what would ye like?

ELLARD. Nothin' either.

BETTY. Ellard.

CATHERINE. Ellard, no. Now, you have some breakfast. I'm supposed to be lookin' after you.

BETTY. What do you want? You can have French toast? Pancakes? What.

ELLARD. Eggs.

BETTY. I thought you didn't *like* eggs. (*Pause.*)

ELLARD. French toast.

BETTY. You can have eggs if you want 'em. I jest thought ye didn't want 'em. You want 'em?

35

ELLARD. Yeah.

BETTY. All *right.* I tell ye, Ellard—these questions ain't that hard. Anybody'd think you 'uz tryin' to make me mad deliberately.

ELLARD. Yes'm.

BETTY. You are?

ELLARD. No'm.

BETTY. All right. How do ye like yer eggs?

ELLARD. (*On the spot.*) What?

BETTY. *How* do ye *like* yer *eggs?*

ELLARD. (*Fearfully.*) They're real good. Thank you.

BETTY. Ellard!

ELLARD. What?

BETTY. When I say, "How do ye like yer eggs," that means, "How do ye want me to fix 'em."

ELLARD. Oh.

BETTY. So how do ye like 'em?

ELLARD. Fried?

BETTY. All *right*, then! (*She storms out.*)

CATHERINE. Ohhh, boy. (*To Charlie and Ellard.*) You two be up for a game of Scrabble later? If I'm not busy makin' some excitin' cookies, or sump'm. Or readin' one of these delightful up-to-date magazines. (*Picking up a ragged magazine and reading.*) "Princess Diana has given birth to a baby boy, her first. The child is as yet unnamed." When *will* she find a name for that baby? (*She drops the magazine and wanders to a window.*) Yeah. Shoot. When is that gal—gonna find a name for that—? (*She has surprised herself with a sudden rush of emotion, which she quietly allays.*)

ELLARD. (*Finally—helpfully.*) Buddy might be good.

CATHERINE. What?

ELLARD. Buddy?

CATHERINE. For what?

ELLARD. That little boy's name?

CATHERINE. (*Dripping with sarcasm.*) Yeah. Prince Buddy. Prince Buddy of England. Be fine. Well. That's settled. I don't know *what* we're gonna do now. We named the prince. Go back to bed, I guess.

ELLARD. That's my favorite name. If I ever catch me that chipmunk, that's what he's gonna be—Buddy the chipmunk.

CATHERINE. Ellard, you couldn't catch a chipmunk if all its

legs were broken and it was glued to the palm of your hand.

ELLARD. I wouldn't want to, then.

BETTY. (*Entering with a tray.*)Here's yer eggs, and they's juice 'n' grits comin' up. (*Handing plates to Charlie and Ellard as she speaks to Catherine.*) Don't ye want coffee, or nothin'?

CATHERINE. No.

BETTY. Toast?

CATHERINE. No!

BETTY. Jest askin'. What you so edgy about today?

CATHERINE. I *am not* edgy.

BETTY. All right. Cain't ask questions in my own house —.

CATHERINE. Not to me you can't, no. You want to ask questions, ask Ellard questions. Don't ask me. All right?

BETTY. (*Looks at Catherine a long moment, then at Ellard, who is eating.*) How d'ye like them eggs?

ELLARD. Fried. (*Betty exits, shaking her head.*)

CATHERINE. Well, I guess I'll go walk down by the lake. (*Exiting.*) Some more. (*And she is gone.*)

BETTY. (*Entering with a second tray.*) Miz Catherine —? Well. (*To Ellard.*) Now, Frog says Charlie don't drink coffee. But if you —. Oh! You wud'n' up last night, was ye? This here's Charlie. Now, he don't understand English none, not hardly even when it's real loud — so don't go tryin' to talk to 'im. You understand?

ELLARD. He dudn' —?

BETTY. No, he's from a foreign country. I don't suppose you never seed a foreigner before?

ELLARD. No'm.

BETTY. (*Expansively.*) No, well, foreigners, once ye get t' know 'em, they's jest reg'lar — blokes.

ELLARD. Uh-huh.

BETTY. Ye get used to all their strange ways, and how they talk, 'n' all. I have. (*To Charlie.*) Ever'thing all right, Charlie? (*Charlie smiles.*) See, now, he didn't hear what I said, really, but he sorta knew, 'cause we got a kind o' extra-circular communication goin', me 'n' him.

ELLARD. Gol-lee.

BETTY. So you behave yerself, now, hear? And don't pay Charlie no mind.

ELLARD. No, I won't (*She leaves them alone. Ellard's idea of paying*

Charlie no mind is to stare at him as though he were a unicorn. Charlie looks at Ellard, smiles. Then he picks up his fork, examines it, frowns. He looks at Ellard, questioning. Ellard looks back, almost responds, but decides not to. Can this stranger really not know what a fork is? No — better to mind one's own business. Ellard eats with his own fork, concentrating self-consciously on his plate. Charlie, studying him, imitates his moves exactly. Ellard's attention is eventually arrested by this phenomenon, and soon, watching each other, they look rather like one person eating before a mirror. Ellard reaches for his orange juice and drains the glass. Charlie, half a move behind, does likewise. Ellard, still watching Charlie, reaches back to replace the glass, but misses the tray, and the glass bounces on the floor. Charlie reaches out and drops his own glass to the floor. He looks at Ellard solemnly, trustingly. Ellard, still watching Charlie, slowly reaches down and retrieves his own glass. Charlie does likewise. They watch each other, motionless. Ellard makes his glass hop through the air like a rabbit. So does Charlie. Ellard looks around. Nobody's seeing this. He puts his glass upside-down over his upheld fork, and twirls it. Charlie does likewise. Ellard puts his glass on his head like a small hat, holding it on with a pointer-finger. Charlie follows suit. Betty enters.)

BETTY. Ellard, what do you call yourself doin'? (*Ellard quickly removes his glass.*)

ELLARD. I don't know. (*Charlie is taking off his glass too.*)

BETTY. No, Charlie, you go on. Put that back up there. (*She "helps" him replace his glass on his head. To Ellard.*) Why was you puttin' that glass on your head, Ellard?

ELLARD. It was — just sump'm we were doin'.

BETTY. *No*, now — you know better than to tell me that. If Charlie wants to put a glass on his head, that's fine. That means — . (*Charlie is trying to sneak his glass down again.*) *No*, Charlie, no. Put it on. That's fine. (*To Ellard, in a more hushed voice.*) That means that's what they *do* in his country, at breakfast time. Evidently they all put *glasses* on their heads. But don't let me catch you doin' it too; that looks like you're makin' fun of him. You hear?

ELLARD. Yes'm.

BETTY. Was that what it was? Was you tryin' to be funny?

ELLARD. No'm.

BETTY. All right, then. (*She stops at the door. Warningly:*) All right — .

38

ELLARD. (*Small.*) I know. . . . (*She nods, exits. Charlie sits there, looking unhappy, finger atop the glass on his head. He looks at Ellard—what should he do now? Ellard considers ignoring him, but Charlie really is too pitiful, sitting there with the glass on his head. Ellard gestures "take it down, now," but Charlie seems not to understand. In a hurried whisper:*) It's all right, take it—you can take it down, now. (*Charlie only looks bewildered. Ellard finally resorts to taking his own glass, putting it atop his head again, then removing it to the table. Charlie does the same.*) Copyin' me. . . . (*They watch each other, still.*) Why in the world—? (*Charlie is frowning again now, having picked up his knife.*) Don't tell me you've never seen a *knife*. (*Charlie looks at Ellard.*) *Knife*. That's a *knife*. Use it to cut things. *Cut* things. (*Mimes.*) Like—ham. If we had some ham. Or bacon, or sump'm. I can't believe you don't—. (*Looks around for help. There is none.*) Or butter. If we had some butter, you could use it to spread it on—. You don't really need it. No, you don't need it. (*Demonstrating.*) Put it down. *Bad*. Uh—. (*Charlie now holds a spoon.*) Yeah, now that's your spoon. Use that to put sugar in your coffee, if you had some sugar, here. And you had some coffee—shoot. I don't really know why we got all these things. But your *fork*—man, I wish somebody else'd help you with this, 'cause I don't know anything, but—I *think* that your *fork*—your fork'd be the main thing you'd use. 'Cause you got your eggs, and you got your grits. Y'see? Eat 'em with a fork, just like we been doin'. (*Shows him. Charlie eats. Ellard watches him eat for a while, then speaks slowly, carefully.*) Can—you—say— "*fork*"? (*Holds up his fork.*) "Faw-werk"? (*Points to Charlie's fork.*) "Faw-werk."
CHARLIE. "Faw. . . ."
ELLARD. "—werk." Two parts. "Faw-werk."
CHARLIE. "Faw . . . werk."
ELLARD. Right. Put 'em together. "Faw-werk."
CHARLIE. "Faw-werk."
ELLARD. Good! That was *great*! (*Charlie smiles tentatively.*) *Yeah*. That was *great*.
CHARLIE. "Faw-werk."
ELLARD. Yeah. (*Pause. Ellard points.*) "*Aigs*"?
CHARLIE. "Aigs"?
ELLARD. Yep. (*Nods.*) Real good.
CHARLIE. "Aigs"?

39

ELLARD. Uh-huh. Let's see — "grits"?

CHARLIE. "Gris"?

ELLARD. "Grits." It's called "hominy grits," really. (*Charlie shakes his head.*)

CHARLIE. "Hom —." (*He shakes his head.*)

ELLARD. That's all right. Grits is fine for now. Just "grits."

CHARLIE. "Grits."

ELLARD. Yeah. That's fine. (*Looking around.*) Let's see, what else? (*Points.*) "Plate"?

CHARLIE. "Plate"?

ELLARD. (*Pointing.*) "Sofa"?

CHARLIE. "Sofa"?

ELLARD. (*Going to the stove.*) "Stove"?

CHARLIE. "Stove"?

ELLARD. "Rug"?

CHARLIE. "Rug"?

ELLARD. (*At the lamp.*) "Layump"?

CHARLIE. "Layump"?

ELLARD. "Bottle"?

CHARLIE. "Bottle"?

ELLARD. "Glass."

CHARLIE. "Glass."

ELLARD. (*Looks around.*) Well — that's all the important stuff in here. You wanna — what do we wanna do now? You wanna —? We could go outside — check out the trees, 'n' stuff? We don't have to, but — we could. Or — yeah. No, let's just take a break, right now. All right? Rest up. An' then we'll check out the trees and all, directly. 'Cause you will, that's, those are all things you'll want to know about, too. 'Cause, like if you ever want to ask somebody, like, where a tree is, or sump'm? Then — you'll want to know that. Or cars? Or chipmunks, or things, 'n' all? All that outdoorsy stuff? But . . . yeah. *Or.* You know what I *could* do. . . . (*As if deciding how to spend ten thousand dollars.*) I could go outside and bring some stuff *in.* I just might do that. 'Cause, since that way we wouldn't — we won't have to go outside, or anything, and we'd have everything right in here where — where we want it. Okay? (*Hopping up.*) All right, you wait here, then. (*Charlie stands.*) No you wait here, I'll be right back. No. *Stay.* (*Charlie stops.*) All right. (*Ellard starts out as Betty enters.*)

BETTY. Where you goin'?

ELLARD. (*Stopping, already breathless.*) Miz Meeks, I'd like to talk, but I'm just real busy right now. (*He exits.*)

BETTY. Laws. (*Going to clear the remains of breakfast.*) You done with yer breakfast, Charlie? You must be. Ye took off your little head-glass. (*Charlie, as if to answer, tears his paper napkin in half.*) That mean yo're done? I reckon it must. (*Experimentally, Charlie stands and, straight-faced, does a brief, wild little dance.*) Ohhh! (*They look at each other.*) That mean ye enjoyed it? (*Charlie does his little smile.*) It does? (*Charlie dances around some more, shading his eyes á la hornpipe, flapping his arms like wings, and doing a fairly complex series of meaningless gestures.*) And—let's see, I don't know if I got all o' that, er not. Sump'm about—was it sump'm about yo're lookin' forward to more o' my cookin'? (*Charlie smiles, watches her.*) And—and ye hope I'll cook ye some chicken? (*Charlie just smiles.*) Well, don't you worry none, Charlie. 'Cause ye know what we're havin' fer dinner this very *night? Chicken!* (*Flaps her arms.*) Yes! Laws, *lawsy*, it's mysterious, ain't it—the way I kin jest read yer brain-thoughts comin' out? I had a pet skunk once, I always knowed jest what he was thinkin' too. He had the same kind o' way of lookin' at me, 'n' all. Yo're jest like him. Yes, sir. (*Charlie puts his hands next to his head and wiggles his fingers.*) Ye *what*, now? Ye—ye want me t' play the harmonica fer ye? Why! How'd you know I used t' play one o' them thaings? Why, that was thirty years ago! Wait right here. (*Betty exits.*)

CHARLIE. (*Laughing.*) Oh, Mary, if only you could see—ha! Ha! (*He begins dancing about again. Catherine enters, sees him, stops. Charlie shoves his hands into his pockets.*)

CATHERINE. Uh-huh! Mind if I sit down here? I am not going up to that yellow room again. Damn picture on the wall of some dogs playin' poker. (*To Charlie.*) Have a seat, what you lookin' at? People in your country bend in the middle? Have a seat. (*Gestures toward a chair. Charlie sits, hands in lap, regarding her.*) That's it. Oh, yeah. This is—this'd be a good place to hang meat. Don't you think? No, we're not supposed to talk to you, I know. (*Pause.*) You don't care. What do you care. (*Pause.*) You starin' at me for? Make me feel like a T.V. set. (*She picks up a newspaper.*) You want the picture section? No? Suit yourself. (*Finding the front page.*) Today's *Constitution,* my goodness. What

41

do we — ? Aww — looky here. Somebody's gone out and torched the Klan headquarters, can you beat that? Up in Atlanta. Yes, sir. Burned the place *down*. That's a switch. Some old boys aren't too pleased right now, you can bet on that. Watch out for them, mister, those Klan boys. They'll get you. You're not a hundred per cent American white Christian, you're liable to find yourself some fine mornin' floppin' around in some Safeway dumpster, minus a few little things. (*Reading elsewhere in the paper.*) Debutante *ball!* Well — look at the little debutantes! Aren't they pretty? Comin' out. (*To the girls in the picture.*) The catch is, girls, you don't get to go back *in*. My, my. (*Absorbed, turning pages.*) What in the world am I doin' . . . . ? I don't know. . . . What else we got here? We got —. (*She says nothing for a moment. Then she puts down the paper and, embarrassed, presses the heels of her hands into her eyes.*) Shoot. 'Scuse me. I don't ever do this. (*Clears her throat.*) I'm just a little bit — weary, this mornin'. (*Clears her throat again.*) I guess? There we go. (*Picks up the paper.*) Uh. . . . (*The paper goes down again, and the hands back over the eyes.*) *Shoot.* (*A long pause.*) I just get sorta — uh — a little sick and tired of things, from time to time. Sometimes I just — I don't know. I don't know. Or what I'm sittin' here jabberin' away at you for, either. You really, you don't understand me at all, do you? That's why, I guess. Talkin' to Betty, or Ellard, you know, there's always that slim little chance you might be understood. Cain't have that. And David, of course, he's off someplace — instead of stickin' around here gettin' to know me. I just keep thinkin' if he — (*An odd laugh.*) if he knew me a little better, he wouldn't —. Ohh, boy. You ever know anybody that — what's your name? Charlie? Charlie. Anybody that was just so good, that you just feel *vile*, most of the time? Yeah. And he is, he's so sweet, and he does for people, and he's so patient. And you get with him awhile, you just realize you've spent your whole life bein' selfish and silly? Doin' dumb things like (*Picking up the paper.*) this, I was one of these little cutie-patooties, 'bout a year ago. Yeah. One year. Lord. Dressin' up, flouncin' around, boppin' all over in my Daddy's plane, sippin' at drinks in revolvin' restaurants. Dumb, dumb, stupid, useless, mindless bullshit. I miss it. I do. I don't think I was cut out to be a decent person. You know? Some people are just meant to be a waste of food, and I think I'm one of 'em. I'm good at it. And a year from now,

42

had off wagon

what? I'm gonna be a mother? Probably own this house? Preacher's wife? I mean—whew! I mean, hold the damn *phone*, a minute. What—how'd all this *hap*pen? You tell me that? Ohhh, Charlie . . . Charlie. I don't know. I guess I just wish things didn't change quite so fast. But . . . they do. They surely do. You got some nice eyes, you know that? You're probably real nice. You're a good listener. You are. Say, "Thank you." (*Pause.*) Hm? "Thank you"? *Warn David*

CHARLIE. Thank you.

CATHERINE. Hey. Thank *you*. (*She pats him on the shoulder.*)

ELLARD. (*Entering with a wheelbarrow full of rocks, hardware, an uprooted bush, etc.*) Here, this ought to hold us for awhile, and then—oh, hey, Cath. Could you scoot over? (*As he wheels the barrow between them.*) Then, uh, I thought of sump'm else we *could* do. We could look at pictures of stuff in books, and that'd be—you know, not quite *as* good, but just about.

CATHERINE. Ellard?

ELLARD. Huh?

CATHERINE. What're you doin'?

ELLARD. We're workin' on some words. He wanted to.

CATHERINE. Oh. . . .

ELLARD. Show you, look. Ready to do some words, Charlie? (*Points.*) What's that?

CHARLIE. "So-fa"?

ELLARD. "Sofa," yep. An' what's that?

CHARLIE. "Rug"?

ELLARD. Uh-huh.

CATHERINE. Well, Ellard?

ELLARD. (*Pointing.*) What's that?

CHARLIE. "Stovva"?

ELLARD. "Stove"?

CHARLIE. "Stove"?

ELLARD. Yeah? That's good.

CATHERINE. Well, Ellard, I declare.

ELLARD. What's this here?

CHARLIE. Ahh. . . .

ELLARD. (*Giving a hint.*) Ends with "Ump."

CHARLIE. "Lay-ump"?

ELLARD. "Layump," that's right.

CATHERINE. Ellard, you taught him to say all these words?

43

ELLARD. Yeah. *harmonica*

BETTY. (*Coming into the room.*) *Woo*-oo! I found it, Charlie! I'd gone 'n' put it away with Meeks's stuff. (*Seeing the others.*) What in the world—?

CATHERINE. Ellard's teachin' Charlie.

BETTY. He *is*?

ELLARD. 'Kay, Charlie, here's some new ones. (*Holding up a rock.*) "Rock"?

CHARLIE. "Rock"?

ELLARD. "Bush"?

CHARLIE. "Boosh"?

BETTY. Well, my land.

ELLARD. "Brick"?

CHARLIE. "Breek"?

CATHERINE. (*To Betty.*) What's that?

BETTY. Oh, Charlie seemed t' want t' hear some harmonica music, so I said—

CATHERINE. You play that?

BETTY. Well—useta could. I think I better go off 'n' practice somewheres, though.

CATHERINE. (*Starting into the kitchen, suppressing a smile.*) My my. A day for surprises.

BETTY. What ye after? Ye need sump'm?

CATHERINE. Just scarin' up breakfast.

BETTY. You are?

CATHERINE. Yeah. (*Catherine exits. A beat. Calling to her:*)

BETTY. You all right?

CATHERINE. (*Off.*) Yes, ma'am.

BETTY. Laws. (*She exits upstairs.*)

ELLARD. All right. Charlie? So what I'm gonna do now, I'm gonna take *allll* these things we just learned, an' I'm gonna mi-i-ix 'em up, okay? (*Catherine, nibbling a muffin, steps back out to watch.*) All right, now, then, no peekin'. Here—. (*He signals Charlie to put his hands over his eyes. Charlie does it. David enters.*) Shhh!

CATHERINE. (*To David.*) Well, look at *you*.

DAVID. Huh? Yeah, I know, I'm a mess. Helpin' to clean up after a fire, down there.

CATHERINE. A fire?

DAVID. Yeah, down the road. Nobody hurt.

44

CATHERINE. That's good.

DAVID. But I'll be gone for a couple of days. (*Seeing the wheelbarrow.*) What's this?

CATHERINE. Come on in here; we're liable to disturb Ellard.

DAVID. What's he doin'?

CATHERINE. English lesson.

DAVID. English—?

ELLARD. 'Kay, Charlie. Hands down. (*Helping him.*) _Down._ All right. Now, wha-at's this?

CHARLIE. "Breek"?

ELLARD. Yeah? This?

CHARLIE. "Boosh"?

ELLARD. Real good.

CHARLIE. Ril good.

CATHERINE. Idn' that sump'm?

ELLARD. This?

DAVID. Well, yes. . . . (*With a grin and a jerk of the head toward the kitchen, Catherine exits.*)

CHARLIE. "Rock"?

ELLARD. "Rock"! Yeah. Okay, some new things. "Jar"? (*Charlie favors David with a big, innocent smile. David returns it, minus a couple of kilowatts.*) Charlie? (*Charlie looks back at him.*) "Ja-ar"?

CHARLIE. "Ja-ar"?

ELLARD. "Nail"?

CHARLIE. "Nail"? (*From another room we hear a sprightly hymn — "Bringing in the Sheaves," perhaps, or "In the Sweet Bye-and-Bye" — being played on the harmonica. David, a little disturbed, turns again to regard Charlie, who has continued with his responses.*)

ELLARD. "Board"?

CHARLIE. "Board"?

ELLARD. "Leaf"?

CHARLIE. "Leaf"?

ELLARD. Together.

BOTH. "Ja-ar"? "Na-ail"? Bo-oard"? Le-eaf"? (*The music continues. David is still watching Charlie. Charlie and Ellard are still reciting, as the lights fade.*)

END OF ACT I

45

H2H - let get seated   [fan] + FOG
LQ33 B/O + House out + SQ10.5
LQ35

Stop sound

Fade complete

ACT II

SCENE 1

Afternoon, two days later. The room is empty. David enters from outside, looks around, then speaks back through the door.

DAVID. All right. (*Owen enters with a corrugated box bound tightly with string.*)
OWEN. Whar is everybody?
DAVID. No tellin'.
OWEN. I still think we oughta do this in the van.
DAVID. No. Let's see what we've got.
OWEN. (*Setting the box down.*) All right. We got all that 'uz left, I think. That 'uz one bad fire.
DAVID. Yep.
OWEN. We 'uz lucky t' get them guns out safe, I tell ye. Them Ruger carbines. I don't guess them books a' yours says too much about Rugers, though.
DAVID. Not much.
OWEN. (*Unfolding a knife and sawing through a bundle of strings.*) Mystery to me how you plan t' take over anything 'thout raisin' a little hell.
DAVID. Don't worry about it.
OWEN. You remember—yo're headin' up this operation fer jest one reason; 'cause you done made us lots a' promises. But I'm warnin' ye—if you don't come up with sump'm right quick—.
DAVID. Don't worry.
OWEN. I mean money. I mean, we need all that money, an' we need ourselves a buildin', an' I mean *now*.
DAVID. We shall have it. Owen, this place is condemned. And just as long as those new bricks don't get used, it stays condemned. We can—.
OWEN. I still think we oughta jest *take* this place. Jest *take* it!
DAVID. (*Stopping him.*) Now, Owen, listen. Listen to me. (*Owen looks at him.*) I tell you, you and I have got an opportunity, here. The whole Georgia empire, what's left of it, it's all out there in that van. The hardware. The uniforms. All of it. We are in such a *position*. And I'll tell you—if you can keep a secret. This time tomorrow, I expect to be a happily-married homeowner.

OWEN. Wha—?

DAVID. True. Quietly, legally. So there's no need to get gun-happy. All right? There's no need to arouse the law, until we are the law.

OWEN. Man, if it wadn't fer that money—!

DAVID. I know. All right. Just think of the money. And calm yourself. (*Referring to the box.*) Let's get this open.

OWEN. (*Opening the box.*) Papers.

DAVID. (*Pulling out ledgers, labels, mailing lists.*) Good. Records, addresses. We need these. Praise God.

OWEN. (*Deeper in the box.*) Boy, howdy. Looky here. (*He extracts a bundle of sticks of dynamite.*) Oh, I do like dynamite.

DAVID. Wait. We just drove up this moutain with a box of dynamite?

OWEN. Don't ye worry. These babies won't go without a charge. These is good little babies.

DAVID. All right, let's put it back. (*Owen obeys.*) Back in the van. Betty goes over this house with a toothbrush. I don't want to have to explain dynamite.

OWEN. All right. (*Picking up the box again.*) Hey, though— (*As they leave.*) how come you didn't tell us you 'uz gettin' married tomorra'? We thought you 'uz gettin' married in November.

DAVID. Oh, Catherine and I just couldn't wait till November.

OWEN. No?

DAVID. No. (*Owen is out. David stops in the doorway, turns back, checking out the room.*) We're too much in love. (*He exits. Presently, from the hallway, we hear Charlie and Ellard clomping down the stairs, and counting as they clomp.*)

CHARLIE & ELLARD. Thirteen, fourteen, fifteen, sixteen, seventeen, eighteen, nineteen—.

ELLARD. (*Bouncing into the room.*) Twenty.

CHARLIE. (*Entering, concentrating.*) Twen-ty.

ELLARD. Now, *how* many stairs are there?

CHARLIE. Twen-ty.

ELLARD. Good. All right. (*Holding up some fingers.*) How many fingers?

CHARLIE. Seex.

ELLARD. Six, yeah. Real good. Now, here's a tricky one. (*Holds up an hourglass.*) How many—little pieces of sand? (*Charlie looks amazed, shrugs.*) A zillion.

CHARLIE. Zeelion?

47

ELLARD. Yeah. When there's just lots of sump'm, you can just say "a zillion."

CHARLIE. A zeelion.

ELLARD. Uh-huh.

BETTY. (*Entering with tray.*) I hoped y'all 'uz comin' back. Here's yer dinners. Grits is on the way.

ELLARD. Don't you rish, now.

BETTY. (*Gratefully.*) I ain't. (*She exits.*)

ELLARD. You doin' real good, though, for just two days' work.

CHARLIE. Thank you. I am happy.

ELLARD. Good. Here. How many chairs?

CHARLIE. Four chairs.

ELLARD. How many fawerks?

CHARLIE. Two fawerks. (*Betty enters with grits.*)

ELLARD. (*To Charlie.*) Good. Real good.

BETTY. (*Serving them.*) Hominy grits!

CHARLIE. A zeelion.

BETTY. What?

ELLARD. No. Nothin'. (*Catherine enters.*)

CATHERINE. Oop! Hey, dinner time, huh? Where've y'all been?

ELLARD. The courthouse, again.

CATHERINE. Hot times in Tilghman, Georgia. Go down 'n' watch 'em build the new courthouse.

ELLARD. Charlie wanted us to.

CATHERINE. How're they comin' with it?

ELLARD. Real good. They let me help, today.

CATHERINE. Well, my *good*ness. They did?

ELLARD. They said I was real — you know, real good.

CHARLIE. Yes, they say good.

CATHERINE. Well, heavens, Ellard.

BETTY. Well, I thought they would. You want some coffee, honey?

CATHERINE. No, I'm all right. I was just gonna draft Charlie into takin' a stroll before dark.

BETTY. 'Nother one 'a yore strolls, huh?

CATHERINE. Oh, yeah. I tell Charlie all my problems, and he just listens . . . and nods . . . you know? Nobody can keep a secret like Charlie can.

48

BETTY. Oh, I think Charlie understands more 'n he lets on.
CATHERINE. (*Laughing.*) Lord, I hope not! I'd be so embarrassed.
BETTY. Well, he's remarkable, anyhow. I know that much.
CATHERINE. Oh, yes, ma'am, no doubt about it. (*Smiling at Charlie.*) Truly remarkable.
CHARLIE. Hm?
ELLARD. "Re*mark*able."
CHARLIE. "Re*mark*able."
ELLARD, CATHERINE & BETTY. Good! (*Froggy enters from outside.*)
FROGGY. Evenin', all.
BETTY. Frog! (*A hug.*)
FROGGY. Lovey.
BETTY. What you doin' up here?
FROGGY. I couldn't stay away, from you flashin' eyes, your perky little nose. Your —.
BETTY. Now, you stop.
FROGGY. I'll try. (*To Catherine.*) 'Ello.
BETTY. Oh, this here's Catherine?
FROGGY. Ah, yes.
CATHERINE. Hello.
BETTY. 'N' Ellard.
ELLARD. (*Shaking hands.*) Hey.
FROGGY. Very nice.
BETTY. This here's Charlie's friend, that brung him up here.
FROGGY. 'At's right. Charlie? (*To Betty.*) 'Ow's it goin', then?
BETTY. Jest grand. Yes, sir. Couldn't be better. Ever'thing's fine.
FROGGY. Really?
BETTY. Yes, indeedy!
FROGGY. But I thought —.
BETTY. Oh, I know. But with Charlie around, ye jest sorta ferget about the bad things, don't ye?
FROGGY. Yer do?
BETTY. Oh, yes. Oh, Frog — you 'uz jest plain wrong, about Charlie. (*To the others.*) He said Charlie was jest gonna be real quiet-like, 'n' reg'lar, 'n' borin'. (*Charlie looks at Froggy, genuinely offended.*)

49

ELLARD. What!

CATHERINE. No!

BETTY. That's what he said! You believe it? (*To Froggy.*) Well, not to us, he ain't. No, sir. Why, I don't reckon a minute goes by, but one of us catches Charlie doin' somethin' er sayin' somethin' real cute an' strange. Wearin' his little head-glass at breakfast?

FROGGY. Wearin' is little wot?

BETTY. No, Charlie ain't borin' at all. No, sir. Charlie, he's — why, he's jest simply — .

CHARLIE. Remarkable. (*Froggy reacts.*)

BETTY. Remarkable. Yes.

FROGGY. Well! (*Smiling, surprised.*) I thought e'd be a bit shy around 'ere. In 'is native country, of course, I know 'e's quite the, eh — the raconteur.

BETTY. The what?

FROGGY. You know — jokes. Amusin' stories. (*Going to the bar for a drink.*) Oh, yes, quite the entertainer back 'ome, they tell me. But 'ere, I thought — .

BETTY. (*To Charlie.*) Oh, tell one!

CHARLIE. (*Falsetto.*) Hm?

BETTY. (*Almost jumping up and down.*) Tell one of yer — . (*To Froggy.*) Make him tell one of his stories!

FROGGY. Oh no, I didn't mean — .

BETTY. Oh, please! Go on, ask him!

CHARLIE. Oh — .

FROGGY. Well — .

BETTY. (*To Ellard and Catherine.*) Y'all listenin'? Charlie's gonna tell one o' his favorite stories! This is the chance of a lifetime! (*To Froggy.*) Go on!

FROGGY. Oh, well — uh, Charlie — ?

CHARLIE. Hm?

FROGGY. Is this all right? I mean, eh — poko dum funnostoros? (*There being no way out, Charlie acquiesces graciously, though nervously.*)

CHARLIE. Ah — blasny, blasny. Eh — .

FROGGY. (*Going for drinks.*) Sorry, mate.

CHARLIE. Eh — . (*Experimentally.*) Brope snyep, snyope ss — . (*Starts over.*) Breez *neez*-nyeep, sneep — . (*No good. Clears throat.*

Froggy hands him a whiskey. He downs it in one gulp, concentrates, and starts — slowly at first.)

Mirduschki omni
  bolyeeshnya,
mirlo aramznyi bro-o-oach
  peevno . . .
(*In a quavering falsetto.*)
"Zhmeetna! Zhmeetna!
Zhmeetna! Zhmeetna!"
(*Narrator voice again.*)
Do—du berznoznia dottsky,
  Marla. . . .
(*With appropriate gestures.*)
Ah! Byootsky dottsky! Perch
  damasa
baxa raxa. Hai.
(*In a silly, youthful falsetto.*)
"Mirlo *meech*no, mirlo em?"

dichni Marla omsk, "y
preeznia praznia, preeznia
praznia, preep?"
"Hai schmotka!" mirlotski
momsk.
"Per dontcha hopni skipni
truda wudsk!"
"Meem? Hopni skipni truda wudsk?
Ha! Ha! Ha! No! No! No!
(*Aside.*)
Heh! Heh! Heh!
(*Aloud.*)
Adios, momsk!"
(*With his left hand, he imitates a skipping youth.*)
Hopni, skipni, hopni, skipni, hopni, skipni truda wudsk.
(*His tone becomes ominous.*)
Meemskivai—omby odderzeiden der foretz, mirduschka—
  *Om*skivar!
(*Deep, decadent, hungry voice.*) .
"Broizhni, broizhni! Broizhni, broizhni!"

("In the little town of
  Merridew
(there lived a little o-o-old
  woman . . .

(*And*—her beautiful
  daughter, Marla. . . .

(Ah! A beautiful daughter!
But as
stupid as a stone. . . .

('I'm heading out now,
  Mom,'
said Marla, 'and trade these
cheeses for some fine
buttons.'"
. . . and so on. . . .)

51

Yach! Aglianastica, Omskivar. Das leetskicheelden ranski haidven Omski's inda vutz.

"Mir-*lo*," Omski deech praznadya. (*Rubbing his stomach.*) "Miro-*lo!* Porlo papno ob*scrod*nyi! Das

(*Imitating with his right hand a huge, slovenly beast crashing through the forest.*)

broizhni, broizhni! Broizhni, broizhni!" Y byootsky dottsky? Hai.

(*Skipping in a semi-circle with his left hand.*)

"Hopni, skipni, hopni, skipni, hopni, skipni—!"

(*Right hand, starting an opposite semi-circle toward the same point.*)

"Broizhni, broizhni! Broizhni, broizhni—!"

(*Left hand.*)

"Hopni, skipni, hopni—."

(*Right hand.*)

"Broizhni, broizhni—."

(*Left.*)

"Hopni, skipni—."

(*Right.*)

"Broizhni—."

(*The two hands confront each other.*)

"Ah?"

(*As Marla, in a fearless—not to say foolhardy—falsetto, chanting loudly.*)

"Irlo mirlo momsky meem! Eevno peevno pomsky *peem!*"

(*A moment—then the right hand, with a snort, gobbles the left and remains alone. Charlie, with a shrug, tells the moral:*)

Blit?

(*The others laugh and applaud.*)

CATHERINE. Well, *Charlie?* You old *story*teller, you.

FROGGY. I don't believe it.

CHARLIE. Thank you.

ELLARD. Charlie, that was real *good.*

CHARLIE. Thank you.

BETTY. An' I understood practically all of it, I think.

CATHERINE. That's funny, I did too, I thought.

BETTY. That part about the tractor? That 'uz *real* clear, to me.

CATHERINE. Tractor?

CHARLIE. Hm?

BETTY. Wadn' there sump'm about a tractor, ridin' around?

52

CATHERINE. Oh, I don't know—.

CHARLIE. Trac-tor?

BETTY. Yeah.

CHARLIE. No.

CATHERINE. No, Betty, I didn't think so. There wadn' any tractor in the story.

CHARLIE. No. Story ees about—beeg machine—to cut ground.

ELLARD. "Big—." Charlie, that *is*. That's a tractor.

CHARLIE. Oh?

ELLARD. Yes!

CHARLIE. Trac-tor! Oh!

ELLARD. Yes!

CHARLIE. Yes! (*To Betty.*) Yes. Story ees about—trac-tor.

BETTY. Ah!

CHARLIE. Yes!

BETTY. I thought I 'uz right about that.

CATHERINE. Well, my goodness.

CHARLIE. Yes. I am sorry.

BETTY. *No*, no, *no*.

CATHERINE. Don't be *sorry*.

CHARLIE. I am bad.

CATHERINE. No!

BETTY. Charlie!

CATHERINE. No, now, don't you even *say* that!

BETTY. Now, *no*, now? Charlie?

CATHERINE. That was a *won*derful story.

ELLARD. It *was*.

CATHERINE. It was *won*derful. You're—*you*—are wonderful. *You.* (*Charlie lowers his head.*) *Yes*!

CHARLIE. (*Sadly and adorably.*) No. . . .

CATHERINE & BETTY. *Yes*!

CATHERINE. Yes, you *are*!

BETTY. You *are*!

CHARLIE. (*Looking up just a little.*) Oh. . . .

CATHERINE. (*Hugging him, laughing.*) Oh, Charlie. Charlie.

BETTY. Look at him.

CATHERINE. My goodness.

BETTY. *Sweet*?

FROGGY. I'm gonna be sick in a minute.

53

BETTY. What?

FROGGY. Nothin'. Well. 'E's picked up a bit of English, I see.

BETTY. Oh, yes. Charlie's been in good hands, all right.

CHARLIE. Last night — I learn — to rid.

FROGGY. Ter "rid"?

CHARLIE. To rid boook.

FROGGY. Ah!

CHARLIE. (*Referring to Ellard.*) He teach me.

FROGGY. Yes. (*To Ellard.*) And 'ow long did it take yer to teach 'im to, uh — ter "rid"?

ELLARD. 'Bout an hour.

FROGGY. One hour, eh?

CHARLIE. Yes! I show you. (*He brings a large volume down from the mantel.*)

CATHERINE. Well, how did I miss this?

CHARLIE. (*With the book open.*) You help.

ELLARD. 'Kay.

CHARLIE. (*Reading.*) "Shall I compare thee to a summer's day? Thou art more lovely — aa — ?" (*He points to a word.*)

ELLARD. (*Helping.*) "And"?

CHARLIE. "And, more temperate." (*To Ellard.*) Yes?

ELLARD. (*After studying the page another moment, and trying to conceal his astonishment at himself.*) Yeah. (*He looks at the page again.*)

CATHERINE. Well, *E*llard? (*Ellard looks at her.*) All that's from just an hour?

ELLARD. Yeah.

CATHERINE. I can't be*lieve* that.

ELLARD. I know. Remember how long it took me to learn to read? 'Bout three years.

FROGGY. Wot d'yer think accounts for the difference?

ELLARD. I don't know. (*Not naming any names.*) I guess he just had a better teacher. (*And it's true, too.*)

FROGGY. (*"I see."*) Ah!

CHARLIE. Yes. (*Speaking of Ellard.*) Remarkable.

CATHERINE. Well. I guess *so*, remarkable. Y'all are right. Pretty soon I'm gonna have to stop talkin' to you, Charlie.

CHARLIE. (*Pointing to her.*) Stop — talk? (*Points to himself.*)

CATHERINE. If you really know what I'm sayin', I can't tell you all my secrets, can I?

CHARLIE. I — I stop learn.

CATHERINE. (*Smiling.*) No, Charlie. (*Squeezing his shoulders.*) No. You go on and learn. Maybe I'll just tell you my secrets anyway.

CHARLIE. Yes?

CATHERINE. We'll see.

CHARLIE. Yes?

CATHERINE. We'll *see.*

CHARLIE. What mean — "We'll see"?

CATHERINE. (*Giving in.*) Oh, it means, yes.

CHARLIE. (*Thoughtfully.*) "We'll see." Mean — yes.

CATHERINE. Yeah. This time it means yes.

CHARLIE. (*To Ellard.*) Een my contry, "yes" ees — "gok".

ELLARD. Gok?

CHARLIE. Gok.

ELLARD. How do you say, "no"?

CHARLIE. Blit.

ELLARD. (*Nods. Pause.*) Blit?

CHARLIE. Gok.

ELLARD. (*Absorbs this.*) Uh-huh.

CHARLIE. (*Offering tea.*) You — would like some?

ELLARD. (*Accepting it.*) Gok. (*Charlie nods. Catherine and Betty whisper and smile at Ellard, who affects not to notice. Ellard offers Charlie some tea.*) You?

CHARLIE. (*Accepting.*) We'll see. (*They sip happily. Froggy wheels away in disgust.*)

BETTY. (*To Froggy, beaming.*) Ain't this nice?

CHARLIE. Froe-gie? Ain't dees nice? (*He imitates Betty's pronunciation — "nahse".*)

FROGGY. (*Turning back.*) Very nice. Gettin' away wiv bloody murder, is wot it is.

BETTY. What?

FROGGY. No, nothin'. I feel a bit dull, myself, but never mind.

BETTY. No, now, Frog. You cain't help it if you ain't a foreigner.

FROGGY. No.

BETTY. Besides, we gotta make the most of Charlie. He's leavin' us tomorra'.

FROGGY. If we can get 'im ter go, yeh. (*Charlie smiles, sips.*)

CHARLIE. La, la. Blasny, blasny.

FROGGY. (*Under his breath.*) "Blasny, blasny." Right.

ELLARD. What's 'at mean? (*Charlie gestures to Froggy — "Go ahead."*)

FROGGY. Wot, "Blasny, blasny"? (*Squinting at Charlie.*) I might be wrong, but I think it means, "Enjoy it while yer've got it." Am I right, Charlie?

CHARLIE. (*The traitor.*) No. "Blasny, blasny"? Eet mean — "Ain't dees nice?"

FROGGY. Ah, yes. Well. Not far wrong, anyway, was I? (*Going to the door.*) Well — I'd like to stay, but I think I'd go mad. So —.

BETTY. (*Regretfully, standing.*) Oh. . . .

FROGGY. Be back tomorrow. (*To Catherine and Ellard.*) Nice to've met yer both. (*A last try.*) Charlie? "Gomo rim jambo."

CHARLIE. (*Who just can't help it.*) "Gomo rim jambo"? (*He looks at the others, shrugs.*) "I sleep with a pheasant"? (*This last line might be reinvented nightly by the actor playing Charlie.*)

FROGGY. (*With a smile of pure malice.*) Ohh, you —.

BETTY. (*At the window.*) Oh, look! It's David.

CATHERINE. (*Joining her.*) David? Well, about time. What's he doin' with that van?

ELLARD. Sellin' vegetables, maybe, from it?

BETTY. What?

ELLARD. Sellin' vegetables? Sometimes people sell vegetables from the backs of those.

BETTY. (*Looks at him for a long beat.*) Well — if you think so, then maybe that's right.

ELLARD. Yeah.

CATHERINE. Well, he's not gonna see me like this. You two keep him out there till I get back down.

BETTY and ELLARD. All right. (*Betty and Ellard leave.*)

CATHERINE. Nice to meet you, Froggy.

FROGGY. Right. (*She exits. Froggy advances on Charlie.*)

CHARLIE. (*Immediately.*) I'm sorry! Something came over me.

FROGGY. Yeh, thanks a lot. Yer made me look like a bleedin' idiot.

CHARLIE. (*Groveling.*) I know, I —. (*Brightening.*) Well, I did, didn't I?

FROGGY. *Yeh!*

56

CHARLIE. I really did. And d'you know what? It wasn't that difficult.

FROGGY. Gor—!

CHARLIE. Nothing to it, really. That gives me an idea!

FROGGY. Oh, yeah? Well, I've got an idea—!

CHARLIE. Oh, Froggy, I'm sorry. I didn't mean to—. I—if only I could tell you what an adventure I've been having! I haven't quite sorted it out myself, yet, but I—Froggy, I think I'm acquiring a personality!

FROGGY. Oh?

CHARLIE. Yes! People here just seem to hand it to me piece by piece as they walk into the room! You see? You just did it too! I—suddenly I'm—a raconteur! And suddenly, I'm Catherine's confessor, and I'm Ellard's prize pupil, and Betty's—pet skunk!

FROGGY. Her wot?

CHARLIE. Oh—. (*Ellard enters from outside. Charlie and Froggy go into doubletalk. Ellard picks up the volume of Shakespeare and goes up the stairs.*) And look. Look! Reading *Shake*speare! Because of *me*, you see? We—all of us, we're becoming—we're making one another complete, and alive, and—oh, I can't explain. But—oh, I shall miss them. I shall miss them terribly.

FROGGY. (*Softening a bit.*) Well—I suppose it's all right, then. I'm late. (*Starts off.*)

CHARLIE. (*Stopping him.*) Froggy. Thank you. Thank you for making me a foreigner.

FROGGY. I feel a bit like Doctor Frankenstein, but never mind. (*Breaks into a wry smile.*) 'Ave yourself a lark. (*He winks and is gone.*)

CHARLIE. (*Pacing furiously.*) Frankenstein. Yes. . . . (*Owen enters.*)

OWEN. (*Quietly, smiling.*) Hey, dummy. (*Charlie turns to him.*) You still here, huh? Well, well. You havin' a nice time? Bet you are. Suckin' around, playin' like yo're one a' us? I tell you one thing, dummy-boy. You enjoy it now. 'Cause I get t' be county sheriff around here—an' I got that Invisible Empire t' back me up—man, they ain't gonna be none o' you left in this county. Foreigners. Yeah. Gonna wipe you all right out—all you dummy boys, black boys, Jew boys. We gonna clean up this whole country, by and by. An' ye know whar it's gonna start? Right here. Thass' right. This' gonna be the most important spot in the U.S. of A., come next couple a' years. It is. You ain't gonna see it, though. No, sir. We gonna ride y'all outta here ever' way they is. Plane. Boat. Yeah, 'n' we can afford it, too. We gonna have lots a' money, real soon. An' you know what I hope? I hope some a' you fights back, too. I jest hope you do. 'Cause I wanna find out what you got fer blood. (*Pause.*)

CHARLIE. (*Brightly.*) Are you happy?

OWEN. (*Stepping back.*) Hey. You *talk*in'.

CHARLIE. (*Singsong.*) Hel-lo. One-two-three. I am happy. Good-bye.

OWEN. (*A derisive snort.*) Oh. . . . (*He gets a hot Coke from the bar, opens it, and watches out the window. Charlie follows him, talking.*)

CHARLIE. One-two-three, G.I.? Beeg-shot, you seestah, one-two-three dollah, upside-down, okay? (*Owen regards him scornfully for a moment, snorts again, and looks back outside.*) Hello, hello! Heap-big dilly-dally, flip-flop, jug-a-rum, big bang theory.

OWEN. What you talkin' about? (*Sits.*) Jabberin'. (*Charlie places himself on the couch opposite him, in lotus position — possibly even upside-down.*)

CHARLIE. (*Same voice.*) Hello! Good-bye! One-two-three. (*Owen snorts, looks away. Pause. Different tone.*) I loook tru your bones. (*Owen looks at him, startled by this. Charlie looks back with ancient eyes and the ghost of a smile.*)

OWEN. (*Finally.*) You say what?

CHARLIE. Yes. Me see. Moon get beeg. You sleep — sleep out, out. All you skin — bye-bye. I come. I look tru your bones.

OWEN. What you talkin' about, mister?

CHARLIE. (*His eyes close.*) Round an' round, and in de town —. (*His eyes open slightly, still looking at Owen.*) Gonna look into your bones, when de *bees* come down. (*Owen watches him, open-mouthed, for another moment, then is instantly at the window.*)

OWEN. Hey! (*Looks back at Charlie, then out the window again.*) Hey! Somebody get in here! Get in here! (*David and Betty enter from outside.*)

DAVID. What's the matter. Owen?

BETTY. What is it?

OWEN. This fella's talkin' crazy.

DAVID. Who is?

OWEN. He is. Talkin' *weird*.

DAVID. Well, he doesn't speak English, remember?

OWEN. Well, he went 'n' *learned* some!

DAVID. What did he say?

OWEN. (*Not taking his eyes off Charlie.*) *Weird* things. Some kinda weird zombie-talk!

DAVID. Like what?

OWEN. I don't *know.* Like all about—(*Trying to recreate the eeriness of the moment.*) about *bees* comin' down.

DAVID. Bees?

OWEN. Yeah. *Bees* comin' down. An'—an' lookin' through *bones,* an'—an' one-two-*three,* an' all.

DAVID. Well, that doesn't sound too bad.

OWEN. Not to you, it don't! He didn't say it right to you! You shoulda seen 'im. His *eyes* got all funny. And they—they was some kinda *rays* comin' out of 'em. They *was.* I *seen* 'em. Some kinda Hoodoo man, thass what I think he is.

DAVID. Now, simmer down, Owen. He seems all right to me.

OWEN. Well, he ain't!

BETTY. Charlie's nice. He wouldn't say nothin' 'bout bees.

OWEN. Yeah, well—"Bees come down," thass what he said. I heared 'im—"*Bees* come down."

DAVID. Well, maybe he did. Still—.

CHARLIE. (*Looking saintly and concerned.*) No. No. (*The others look at him. He places a kindly hand on Owen's shoulder.*) "Please—calm down."

DAVID. "Please calm down." That's what he was saying, Owen. Not "Bees come down." I think that's good advice, too. (*Owen watches Charlie like a serpent.*)

BETTY. I knowed it was sump'm like that.

OWEN. He said, "Bees come down."

DAVID. Owen—"Bees come down" doesn't make any sense.

OWEN. I know that! Thass why I 'uz brangin' it to yer attention!

DAVID. All right, Owen.

OWEN. An' don't talk to me like that! "All right, Owen." Talk to me like I 'uz some half-wit kid, er sump'm.

DAVID. All right. (*Catherine enters from upstairs, having prettied up some.*)

CATHERINE. Well, looky who's here. The young Reverend David Marshall Lee, as I live and breathe. My, my—decided to make an appearance, did we, after bein' gone for a whole day?

DAVID. (*A little surprised.*) I've been gone for two days.

CATHERINE. (*Surprised herself.*) Oh. . . .

BETTY. He brung home a purty little green van, too.

DAVID. That's right. The company that burned down, you know, in Atlanta? They were so grateful to me and Owen for our help, they've lent me their Volkswagen van for my ministry until they rebuild. Isn't that something?

CATHERINE. (*Looking out the window.*) Very nice.

DAVID. It's a much-needed gift, I'll tell you that. Right out of the ashes. Praise God. (*He smiles at the company.*)

BETTY. Ellard figgered you 'uz gonna sell vegetables from it.

DAVID. Well, that's Ellard. (*He looks down with a grin and a shake of the head. Perhaps he is aware that no one joins him.*)

ELLARD. (*Entering.*) Hey.

CATHERINE. Hey, bro.

BETTY. Ellard here's been teachin' Charlie English.

DAVID. (*To Ellard.*) Well, did you continue with that? That's fine.

ELLARD. Yeah.

DAVID. Teaching him various words, and so on, were you?

ELLARD. Yeah.

DAVID. Well, that's good. That's just fine. (*He smiles at Charlie.*) He — ? Ellard — teach — you?

CHARLIE. Indubitably. (*Everyone is surprised by this. Charlie turns to Ellard for confirmation.*) Yes?

ELLARD. (*A little dazed, but rising to the occasion.*) Yeah. Real good.

CATHERINE. Ellard!

CHARLIE. (*With an effort at first, then gathering momentum.*) He — teach —. (*Correcting himself.*) He — has taught — me ⁻many — new words. (*Everyone watches Charlie.*) Conseedering eet has only been two days.

CATHERINE. Why, *E*llard! That is amazing!

CHARLIE. (*Verifying it with Ellard as he speaks.*) Tomorrow — we study — prepositional phrases. Yes?

ELLARD. Well, we might. Yeah.

CATHERINE. I don't be*lieve* this, Ellard. David, can you believe all this?

DAVID. (*Still cool and sweet.*) Well, *no*, I — it's *hard* to believe, isn't it?

CATHERINE. (*To Ellard and Charlie.*) You two—first that courthouse business, and now this?

DAVID. What?

CATHERINE. Oh, Charlie's been takin' Ellard to watch 'em build the new courthouse. And you know what? They've got Ellard learnin' how to lay bricks.

DAVID. What?

OWEN. What?

CATHERINE. Yeah. I guess he's gettin' compliments from the workers, and everything.

CHARLIE. Yes. (*Owen glares at David.*)

CATHERINE. (*To Ellard and Charlie.*) All these achievements, I think we oughta have a party, or sump'm.

OWEN. (*Through his tooth.*) Yeah. (*To David.*) Surprise party, maybe.

DAVID. Owen?

CATHERINE. Or you know what? I know what. Listen, y'all! (*To Ellard.*) Ellard, do you know what I'm gonna do?

ELLARD. Unh-unh.

CATHERINE. By God, I'm gonna give you your inheritance!

ELLARD. What?

DAVID. Catherine—?

CATHERINE. I am. Daddy told me if I ever thought you were smart enough to handle it, I was to give you half the family money—a hundred and twelve thousand dollars.

ELLARD. Gol-*lee.*

OWEN. (*To David.*) Jest stand there, why don't ye.

DAVID. (*Big smile, going to Catherine.*) Honey! That's *wonderful* of you! Even better, I'll tell you what—right after we're married, we'll have a big celebration, and we can present the check to him together.

CATHERINE. All right!

DAVID. Good.

CATHERINE. We've got Charlie to thank, really.

DAVID. Yes! I'd like to find out more about you, Charlie. Tell me—.

CHARLIE. Gok?

DAVID. You—. What?

CHARLIE. Gok?

61

ELLARD. Means "yes".

DAVID. Oh, I see. "Gok."

CHARLIE. Gok.

ELLARD. And "no" is "blit". (*Pause. David nods. Is he going to say it?.*)

DAVID. "Blit"?

ELLARD & CHARLIE. Gok. (*Pause. David looks at Ellard, then back at Charlie.*)

DAVID. All right. Uh, Charlie, now—where is it that you're from?

CHARLIE. From?

DAVID. Yes—uh, your *home*. What is the *name*, of your home?

CHARLIE. Charlie house. (*Catherine and Betty whisper and smile.*)

DAVID. No. I mean, where do you live? (*Charlie shakes his head. More slowly.*) *Where*, do you *live*? (*Charlie looks to Ellard.*)

ELLARD. Where do you live at?

CHARLIE. Where do I live at! Ah! I show you. Do you hev glob?

DAVID. Do I have glob?

CHARLIE. Glob! Glob of world!

DAVID. Oh. Uh, no, I don't believe we do.

CHARLIE. Then—? (*He shrugs.*)

DAVID. We might have an atlas, though, or something. Betty?

BETTY. (*Who has already started looking.*) Here's a map. (*Unfolding it.*) Well, it's jest of Georgia.

DAVID. Well—.

CHARLIE. Ees good. I show you. (*Looking at map.*) Hmm. (*Hands the map, facing us, to Owen.*) Here. Please hold.

DAVID. (*Seeing Owen's reluctance.*) Come on, Owen. Just hold the map, please, all right? (*Owen holds it grimly.*) All right.

CHARLIE. (*Studies map.*) So. You leev—(*Pointing.*) here?

DAVID. Yes?

CHARLIE. So. I leev—(*He stands back from the map, getting a bearing on it. He seems to be calculating a location somewhere to the right of it. To Owen, motioning him away and to Charlie's left.*) Go. Go. (*Owen, with a scowl, moves farther back and left, still holding up the map. Charlie now is alternating looks at the map with looks at a vague area far R.*) Go. (*Owen is against the back wall now, near the outer door. Charlie still seems unsatisfied. To Owen.*) Out. Go out. (*Owen*

62

looks at David, who nods, motioning him out. Owen goes out the door and stands outside the window. Charlie motions him to go even farther away, and Owen disappears from view completely. David stands by the window. Charlie motions Owen to go farther still, and the gesture is relayed by David. Finally, satisfied, Charlie selects a spot in the air far R. and about eight feet off the ground. He points to it.) Here.

DAVID. *(At door, disgusted.)* Come back in, Owen.

CHARLIE. *(To the others, proudly.)* My home.

BETTY. Looks like a nice place to live. *(David looks at her a long moment. Owen reenters, not happy. He looks around.)*

OWEN. What the hell was I doin' out thar?

BETTY. I don't know. We 'uz all in here, lookin' at Charlie's home.

DAVID. Never mind, Owen.

OWEN. Never mind!

DAVID. *(Looking at Charlie.)* I was trying to find out some details about Charlie, but apparently that's going to be difficult.

CHARLIE. Hello.

DAVID. Charlie, what — what language do you speak?

CHARLIE. What — language?

DAVID. Do you speak.

CHARLIE. Do I speak?

DAVID. Yes.

CHARLIE. Yes. Hello.

DAVID. No. No. What — what is your tongue?

CHARLIE. "Tongue"!

DAVID. Yes, what — what *name* do you have for your *tongue?*

CHARLIE. "Floppy." *(Pause.)*

DAVID. *"Floppy."*

CHARLIE. Yes, Floppy de tongue. *(Pause.)* What name you have for *your* tongue?

DAVID. *(Still incredulous.)* *"Floppy"!*

CHARLIE. Same as mine! Ah!

DAVID. *(Regrouping.)* Uh — .

CHARLIE. Remarkable!

CATHERINE. David — why don't you have Ellard help you?

DAVID. *(Controlling his anger at this suggestion.)* All right.

ELLARD. *(To Charlie.)* He wants to know about your kin'a talk.

CHARLIE. My kin'a talk! *(For example.)* "Gok"? "Blit"? Yes?

63

ELLARD. Yeah.

CHARLIE. Yes. Yes. (*David sighs.*) I teach.

DAVID. What?

CHARLIE. I teach to you.

DAVID. No—.

CHARLIE. No?

DAVID. No. That wasn't what I—.

CHARLIE. No? My kin'a talk—bad?

DAVID. What?

CHARLIE. Ohh. I am bad?

CATHERINE. No, Charlie.

CHARLIE. (*Sadly.*) Oh. . . .

CATHERINE. David, for Lord's sakes.

DAVID. What?

CATHERINE. You've hurt his feelings.

DAVID. Hurt his feelings?

CATHERINE. Yes.

DAVID. What about me? What about my feelings?

CATHERINE. *Da*vid.

DAVID. I *mean* it.

CATHERINE. Just try to get along with him, that's all.

DAVID. I'm trying to get along! I asked him stuff, didn't I? Asked him about himself. What did I find out? His tongue is named Floppy, and he lives in the air!

CATHERINE. David.

DAVID. It's a little frustrating, you know. Grant me that.

CATHERINE. No, it isn't. You have to be patient.

DAVID. Patient! You're telling me how to be *pa*tient?

CATHERINE. David.

DAVID. Who the hell are you to tell—!

CATHERINE. I've never seen you like this.

ELLARD. (*The forgiving soul.*) Maybe it's just a phase.

DAVID. All right. What do you want? You want me to learn some words from this man?

CATHERINE. Well, yes. Look at him. He really just wants to give us something, can't you see that?

CHARLIE. (*Earnestly, to David.*) Yes. I really want geev eet to you.

DAVID. All right.

CHARLIE. Yes? I teach now?

64

DAVID. (*Summoning up his calm again.*) Yes. Why don't you teach me something?

OWEN. (*Moving toward the door.*) Well, don't that jest cut it? Do anything she says, I reckon, wouldn't ye? I reckon if she said fer you to—.

DAVID. Owen, we can discuss this later.

OWEN. Ain't gonna be nothin' to discuss. Not once I go down into town 'n' tell some friends of mine who's up here shinin' up to foreigners.

DAVID. Owen—if you'd think about it, maybe you'd realize why I'm doing this.

OWEN. I can see why.

CATHERINE. Who cares, David? Let him go.

DAVID. No, honey. (*Looking at Owen.*) Owen is one of God's children too. I think he might profit from a lesson as much as any of us. (*To Owen.*) I think you should stay. And join me in this.

OWEN. I ain't stayin' here talkin' no damn Hoodoo talk!

DAVID. (*Evenly.*) Owen. You must learn to be meek. Otherwise you may never inherit the earth. (*Pause. Then, to nearly everyone's surprise, Owen pulls up a chair and sits, fuming.*)

CATHERINE. I'm not sure what you just did.

DAVID. (*Putting an arm around her shoulders.*) I just doubled the size of Charlie's class, honey. (*She looks at him.*)

CHARLIE. I teach now. (*Motioning them all to join.*) All.

BETTY. All of us? Well—.

CHARLIE. All say. "Gok. Blit."

ALL. (*Except Owen.*) "Gok. Blit."

CHARLIE. (*Points to Owen.*) You say—"gok"? (*Owen looks around, grim. Patiently.*) "Gok"? (*Pause.*)

DAVID. Go on, Owen. It's not going to hurt you. We're sharing something, here.

CHARLIE. (*Gently, to Owen.*) Yes. We share. (*Patiently.*) "Gok"? (*Long pause.*)

OWEN. (*Finally.*) "Gok."

CHARLIE. HA! Hahahahahahahahahahahahahaha! You say eet like *wo*-man! (*Holding his sides, sliding down in his chair.*) HA! Hahahahahahaha!

OWEN. (*Standing.*) Look here, you little—!

DAVID. (*Standing.*) Have a seat, Owen. (*They both sit.*)

65

CHARLIE. (*Still weeping with laughter.*) I am sorry, but — sound so stupid!
DAVID. All right.
CHARLIE. (*Imitating Owen.*) "Gawk"! Hahahahahahahahaha!
(*Catherine, watching Charlie, is starting to laugh too.*)
DAVID. Honey?
CATHERINE. I'm sorry. I've just never seen him so tickled.
CHARLIE. I am sorry.
CATHERINE. Don't be sorry.
CHARLIE. Yes. Yes. I am sorry. (*Things are on the verge of set-tling down again, when Ellard bursts out with a guffaw.*)
OWEN. (*Standing.*) All right!
DAVID. Owen!
OWEN. I don't have to put up with this!
DAVID. Owen, nobody's laughing at you.
OWEN. The hell they ain't!
DAVID. Ellard, now what were you laughing at?
ELLARD. (*Sobering himself.*) Just — sump'm I made up.
DAVID. All right. (*To Owen.*) All right, Owen? (*Now Betty bursts out laughing. Trying not to sound irritated.*) Betty? What is it?
BETTY. (*Through laughter.*) Jest — sump'm Ellard made up!
(*Everyone but David and Owen laughs.*)
DAVID. Catherine, maybe we'd better just cease this. This idea of a lesson.
CHARLIE. No! No! I teach. Ees important lesson.
CATHERINE. Oh. . . .
CHARLIE. Yes?
BETTY. Oh, David, let 'im go on.
CATHERINE. David, now, we'll be good.
DAVID. (*Against his better judgement.*) All right.
OWEN. Not me.
DAVID. Owen — .
OWEN. He called me stupid. Nobody calls me stupid.
DAVID. I'm sure he didn't mean — really, *stupid.*
CHARLIE. No. No. Een my country — stupid — *good.*
OWEN. What?
CHARLIE. We have saying — "When you not sure — ask a stupid person. Then do something else."
OWEN. What the hell's 'at s'posed to mean?

BETTY. I think *I* understood it!

DAVID. Betty.

OWEN. Does that —? Man, I got half a mind to —.

DAVID. Owen?

CHARLIE. He have half a mind? (*As if that explained things.*) Ah.

DAVID. Charlie. (*Owen glares.*)

CHARLIE. (*Back to the lesson.*) So — "gok, blit." (*To Ellard.*) How you say, "Yes"?

ELLARD. "Gok."

CHARLIE. Good! (*to Catherine.*) How you say, "No"?

CATHERINE. "Blit"?

CHARLIE. *Ril* good! (*to David.*) How you say, "I go to chop wood today"?

DAVID. Uh — I don't know.

CHARLIE. (*Patiently.*) "I go — to chop wood — today."

DAVID. Uh —. (*Looks at the others.*)

CHARLIE. Try.

DAVID. I don't know.

CHARLIE. (*Sighs, turns to Betty.*) You try.

BETTY. (*Immediately.*) "Dooley dooley"?

CHARLIE. "Dooley dooley." Yes. (*Betty nods, no longer surprised at her powers.*)

DAVID. (*Frustrated.*) Wuh — how did she know that?

CHARLIE. (*Hands on hips, right into David's face.*) She pay attention!

OWEN. What the hell!

DAVID. Owen! Remember. The other cheek.

CHARLIE. (*Happily.*) Yes, yes, other cheek, Owen — other cheek and half a mind.

OWEN. (*Turning on him.*) You shut up! Jest *can* it, mister! I done took all I'm gonna take from you, now! Settin' around here, talkin' this monkey-jabber! The hell do you think I am?

DAVID. Owen —.

OWEN. (*Pulling out his knife.*) Shut *up*, I said! All a' you! Y'all jest thought ye'd mess with me, did ye? 'Zat it? Huh? Have a little fun with some dumb cracker? 'Zat what you 'uz thinkin'? Huh? Well, you gonna find out who's the dummies around here!

DAVID. Will you —?

67

OWEN. *Cut* it! Book-man! I'm doin' the talkin' from now on! Me! I got me some friends down thar—they don't think I'm so dumb. Matter fact, they jes' waitin' t' hear one word from me—jest one little word, before they come ridin' up this mountain in a blaze a' light! Ridin' out, the way they been doin' fer a hunnerd years! More'n a hunnerd years! Takin' care of foreigners like him. So you get yerselves ready. (*To Catherine and Betty.*) Put on yer pretty dresses, women. You fixin' to meet the Klan. (*He exits. The others watch after him. We hear the sound of an engine roaring off down the mountain.*)

DAVID. That was unfortunate. That was really unfortunate.

CATHERINE. The Klan. Was that what he said? The *Klan*?

DAVID. Yes! Yes, that's what he said.

CATHERINE. Is Owen with the *Klan*?

DAVID. I don't know, how do I know?

CATHERINE. Well—?

DAVID. I'm going after him.

CATHERINE. What? Don't go after him. Why don't we just—?

DAVID. Will you stop? Will you *stop*? Look—Owen is—I think he's deeply troubled. I've been trying to work with the man.

CATHERINE. David! Don't you get it? He's threatening us. I'm gonna call the police.

DAVID. No!

CATHERINE. (*At the phone.*) What?

DAVID. You've helped enough.

CATHERINE. What?

DAVID. Don't call the police. Let me do this. Please! Let me try to salvage this. *Please!*

CATHERINE. Well—?

DAVID. Don't call the police (*And he is gone.*)

CATHERINE. (*Still watching after him, stunned.*) He doesn't know who he's dealing with. Those Klan boys. (*We hear David's car driving off.*)

BETTY. Oh, they wouldn't come up here.

CATHERINE. Betty, they will. If it's really the Klan, all Owen has to tell 'em is that Charlie's up here. That's all the excuse they need for about forty of 'em to get boozed up and grab their guns and come whoopin' up here, with their damn sheets over their heads.

CHARLIE. Sheets? Over heads?

68

CATHERINE. That's how they do, yeah. They put sheets over their heads, and—. Oh, Charlie. You have no idea what we're talkin' about at all, do you?

CHARLIE. No.

CATHERINE. (*Almost laughing.*) Whoo! You didn't know what you were gettin' us into with that language lesson of yours.

CHARLIE. I?

CATHERINE. Yeah, well, you're not to blame. You were just bein' yourself.

CHARLIE. (*Feeling terrible.*) Oh. . . .

CATHERINE. But we've gotta—. Oh, why'd I promise we wouldn't call the police? Who else? Who do people call—the Army?

CHARLIE. The Army.

CATHERINE. Or the Marines?

CHARLIE. Froe-gie!

CATHERINE. Yeah, all right, call Froggy. (*Charlie dials.*) I doubt that he's back yet, but who else? Neighbors, or old friends? Or—?

BETTY. I'm tryin' t' think who all ain't dead.

CATHERINE. Yeah.

BETTY. Fred 'n' Marvin Dowdle, could try them. Or old Man Reed.

CATHERINE. Maybe we just oughta call the police.

BETTY. Ezzard Purkeypile'd come up, I know. 'Course, he's missin' both arms.

CATHERINE. Let's call the police.

CHARLIE. (*On the phone.*) Hel-lo! Hel-lo! (*Confused, handing receiver to Catherine.*) Eet—.

CATHERINE. (*Listening.*) Answering machine. Great. Come on. Yeah, this is Catherine Simms, up at Betty's? Listen, Froggy, we might be in trouble. There might be some men with guns on their way up here. I don't think they like foreigners too well. If you could just, I don't know, bring anyone, bring anything you can. And if you run into a mean-lookin' fella drivin' a green van, that's Owen Musser. Kick a hole in his tire, or sump'm, will you? We're callin' the cops, so there's probably nothin' to—\ Hello? We've been—hello? We've been cut off. LQ39 blue

BETTY. Let me see.

CATHERINE. Ellard, try the lights. (*He does. Nothing.*)

69

BETTY. (*Into phone.*) Hello?

CATHERINE. Betty, they've cut off our electricity.

BETTY. What?

CATHERINE. They've cut the electricity off—down at the road, or somewhere. Now that scares me.

BETTY. That does sound right bad, don't it?

CATHERINE. Yeah. They're not just foolin', now. It's gonna be dark soon, too.

BETTY. They better *not* come up here. Tearin' away at this house, er tryin' t' scare Charlie.

CATHERINE. Well—David's down there, I know, but listen—if we should have to defend ourselves—what've we got?

BETTY. (*Searching the walls.*) Ol' Meeks wouldn't allow no guns in here. Had enough of 'em in the war, he said.

CATHERINE. Ellard? Help us think.

ELLARD. Me?

CATHERINE. I just gave you a hundred thousand dollars for bein' smart. You're the highest-paid mind we got here, now. *Think* of sump'm.

ELLARD. (*Finding a croquet mallet.*) Hey, how 'bout this?

CATHERINE. Yeah.

BETTY. Charlie! (*Charlie looks at her.*) Charlie! I 'uz plumb fergettin' we had *you* here!

CHARLIE. (*Frozen.*) Hah?

BETTY. You tell us what to do! You been all over the world! You got all them mysterious ways o' doin' things, an' all!

ELLARD. Oh, yeah, I bet Charlie will come up with sump'm.

CHARLIE. Ohhh. . . . (*"I don't think so."*)

CATHERINE. Any idea you have, Charlie. Even a stupid one, at this point.

CHARLIE. (*Looking around.*) Stupid idea. Stupid idea.

CATHERINE. It dudn' *have* to be stupid. Just—.

BETTY. He's got an idea right now. I can always tell.

CHARLIE. (*Sickly.*) Oh . . .

CATHERINE. Charlie, if you do, if you have any kind of idea, please tell us.

CHARLIE. (*Still in dialect, though perhaps he doesn't realize it.*) Listen, I . . . I'm not—. (*He is on the verge of confession, but suddenly his attention is arrested by something in the center of the floor. The others look, too. The throw-rug? He looks at the mallet in Ellard's hands, and*

70

back at the spot on the floor. He picks up the rug and tosses it aside, still watching the spot.)

CATHERINE. Charlie? What—what are you thinking? (*Pause.*) Charlie?

CHARLIE. (*Looks at the spot for another second, then up at Catherine. Pause.*) "Sheets"?

CATHERINE. What? (*Charlie looks at Betty. Then he looks back at Catherine. He does not speak again.*)

LQ 41 BLACKOUT

LQ 43 Blue

double 60

LQ 45 LUP SQ 16.2

ACT II

SCENE 2

Fade

The calm before the storm. Outside the window, darkness. Within, a candle or two illumine the figures of Catherine, who stands vigil at the window, and Charlie, on the couch.

CATHERINE. I'm not going to worry any more. I'm just not. They would have been here by now. I think the electricity went off by itself, and I think David's down there with Owen right now, swappin' jokes. Or prayin' together, or something. Well, maybe not that. But I bet there's nothin' to worry about any more. So don't worry.

CHARLIE. No. Worry ees the uncle of despair.

CATHERINE. Is that what y'all say in your country?

CHARLIE. Yes.

CATHERINE. Tell me sump'm about your country, Charlie. Anything. Tell me what it's like.

CHARLIE. (*Who seems genuinely troubled by this.*) Ees deeficult. Eet ees—so long ago.

CATHERINE. Only two days, Charlie. That's all.

CHARLIE. (*Frowning.*) Hm.

CATHERINE. Are you married, or anything?

CHARLIE. Yes.

CATHERINE. What's her name?

CHARLIE. . . . Mavra.

CATHERINE. Mavra. That's pretty.

71

CHARLIE. Yes. She ees — ill.

CATHERINE. Oh, I'm sorry. Do you love her a lot?

CHARLIE. Yes.

CATHERINE. And what all do you do? Do you — do you take walks together?

CHARLIE. Yes. (*Pause.*) Some time we take walks apart.

CATHERINE. Uh-huh. And do you — have lots of friends? (*He nods.*)

CHARLIE. Yes. (*Pause.*) She have — twenty-three.

CATHERINE. Twenty-three?

BETTY. (*Entering from stair.*) Any sign o' company?

CATHERINE. No.

BETTY. Well, I done what Charlie said — took out all the lightbulbs upstairs. So's even if the electricity comes back on, it'll still be dark as pitch up thar.

CATHERINE. Well, I'm hopin' the danger's past.

BETTY. Don't say that to Ellard. He wants to try out Charlie's plan.

CATHERINE. Now, did we lock that front door?

BETTY. I'll get it. (*A crash at the front door puts Catherine on her feet. But it is only Ellard, dusting himself off as he enters.*)

ELLARD. Just me.

CATHERINE. I am still a little jumpy, I guess.

ELLARD. I got that thing rigged up again. We wanta practice once more?

CATHERINE. No, why'n't you just stay in here awhile, okay?

ELLARD. 'Kay. I think we got it, anyhow.

CATHERINE. All right, now, think — (*Trying to be optimistic.*) just think. If they did come up here, what's the worst — the worst that could happen?

ELLARD. They could kill us. Then they could cut us up into little pieces and hang us from some trees.

CATHERINE. You're thinkin' too much, Ellard.

ELLARD. That's what I get paid for.

CATHERINE. Look at this commando group. We got, what — a foreigner? An ex-deb? A nice old lady? And a wealthy, bricklayin' English teacher. I don't see how we could lose, do you? Shoot. An' a cro*quet* mallet. (*Laughs.*) Hoo-ee. How entirely stupid.

CHARLIE. Also — we have stupid plan.

CATHERINE. That's right. Stupid plan, stupid croquet

mallet. We're *set*.

ELLARD. What's wrong with my croquet mallet?

CATHERINE. Oh, nothin'.

ELLARD. I thought it was—good?

CATHERINE. Well, it'd sure give us a chance to find out how brave we all are.

CHARLIE. (*Who has been having similar thoughts.*) Yes. *Highon*

CATHERINE. Now, Betty—my guess would be that Betty— (*She stops, having seen something out the window.*)

BETTY. What is it, hon?

CATHERINE. I think I saw a headlight through the trees. (*Pause.*) Yep. *18 SQ - about crowd*

BETTY. (*Going to the window.*) Maybe it's David. Er Frog. (*Pause. An orange glow lights their faces.*)

CATHERINE. Nope. (*Charlie stands.*) Are we locked up? We can do that, anyway.

BETTY. I'll get it. (*She goes to the door and locks it.*)

ELLARD. (*Suddenly afraid.*) Is it them?

CATHERINE. Yeah, it's them. I can see their damn torches. They'll be up here in no time. There's the van.

BETTY. Y'all better get upstairs.

CATHERINE. Yeah. Come on, El. (*But Ellard just stands there, frozen.*)

ELLARD. They gonna—?

CATHERINE. Don't think about it, El. Come on.

ELLARD. I—.

CATHERINE. Come on, El. If we're gonna *do* this.

ELLARD. I—.

BETTY. What's wrong, Ellard?

CATHERINE. He's scared.

ELLARD. (*Looking at his mallet.*) If it's stupid. They're gonna—.

CATHERINE. No, don't think about that. We don't have any *choice*. Let's *go*.

ELLARD. I—.

CATHERINE. (*Trying to herd him out, and failing.*) I can't get him to—.

CHARLIE. (*To Ellard, improvising wildly.*) Leesten! Thees—. Eet—croquet mallet! Een my contry, croquet mallet ees great seembol of—of—of—*frid*dom!

ELLARD. Huh?

73

CHARLIE. Yes! And—and we hev king. Great, famous, famous—uh—. (*Outside, in the distance, we hear sounds—car horns, and Indian whoops, and an occasional rifle shot.*)

CATHERINE. Charlie—.

CHARLIE. Famous, uh—*warrior*! Warrior king! Very brave! Many bettles he ween weeth—croquet mallet!

ELLARD. Huh?

CHARLIE. Yes! Ulways fight weeth croquet mallet! Here! Hold! (*Racing against time now, he raises the mallet in Ellard's hands to a passably regal position.*) Ah! De *same*! De *same*! You loook like heem!

ELLARD. (*Tentatively.*) The king?

CHARLIE. Yes! Yes! De *king*! De *king*! (*Ellard looks at the mallet, still not convinced. Desperately.*) King Buddy!

ELLARD. (*Scarcely able to believe it.*) King *Bud*dy?

CHARLIE. Yes!

CATHERINE. Charlie—.

CHARLIE. Yes! (*There is a loud thud, as something pushes against the front door. The firelight on Charlie's face grows brighter as he proclaims above the din.*) Yatskavnia pridotsk! Yatskavnia strachnia balnibarbi, ambo atarashi hon! Sturm und drang, prasny! La guerra civil! Solamente les enfants du paradis!

ELLARD. What's 'at mean?

CHARLIE. Et mean—"Separately, we are all single people. But together, we are as four!"

BETTY. That's what I think, too.

ELLARD. Let's go get 'em! (*Ellard rushes out the stairway entrance.*)

CATHERINE. (*To Charlie.*) "King Buddy"? Charlie, how did you know—?

CHARLIE. Go. Go! (*She looks at him for another second. Then she is gone. The door crashes open offstage. The sound of wind. The candles flicker and go out. Darkness and silence. Then the sound of heavy shoes—many of them, coming into the room. A flashlight beam picks up the faces of Betty and Charlie, and grows closer and brighter. Outside, engines, murmurs, the glow of torches. Inside, boots, the swish of robes, the heavy click of slung weapons. Again, all comes to a stop. Betty looks into the light.*)

OWEN. (*On a hand-held loudspeaker.*) Are you the owner of this house?

74

BETTY. You know I am.

OWEN. *Are you prepared this night to stand before the holy tribunal of the Invisible Empire?*

BETTY. I never done you harm, Owen.

OWEN. *Are you prepared, woman, to stand this night before the holy tribunal of the Invisible Empire?* (*No Answer.*) *I'm giving you your chance to answer.* (*No answer.*) *Is this here the foreign man that you been harborin' up here? Are you aware of the crime against our people for which you stand liable and accused? Speak!*

BETTY. Charlie ain't done nothin' wrong, an' you know it.

OWEN. (*Putting the loudspeaker down.*) All right! Y'all heard her! She admits this is him. This is the man we want. Gimme that walkie-talkie. (*Into the walkie-talkie.*) All right, Billy. Cut the lights back up. (*The lights come back on, and we can see what was only visible in silhouette before — a gang of men in white robes, some carrying weapons — shotguns, pistols, army rifles. All are hooded. Owen's high rank is designated by colorful insignia sewn onto his own hood. Note: A really audacious budget production might have the actors playing David, Froggy, Catherine and Ellard throw on robes and boots the moment they are offstage, run around to the outer-door entrance and come back on as Klansmen. It's an appealing notion to think of what seems to be a stage full of new characters actually being played by the same cast we have seen all evening, five of them now in sheets. In such case, probably the actors playing Ellard, Catherine, and David would be dispatched upstairs, leaving the actor who plays Froggy to keep Owen company below.*) This here's the Invisible Empire. Standin' right here. Take a good look at us, Charlie-boy. We gonna take care a' you fer awhile. (*To Betty.*) Yes, ma'am. We gonna take Charlie off yer hands. Treat him real nice, too, on account a' he's gonna be our hostage. An' you know what the rest a' you's gonna do? Jest disappear. You gonna get escorted down to that highway *right* now. You gonna get on that first Trailways bus outta here, and nobody's gonna hear from you again, 'cause if'n we do, then Charlie here's gonna get to see what his innards look like. This here's the *Klan*, y'all! Y'all don't *fool* with the *Klan*! Whar's them others at? The girl, an' her kid brother? Whar *are* they? (*No answer. To some of the Klansmen.*) Check out the house, y'all. (*Four of the Klansmen run upstairs.*) Yeah, let's get ever'body down here. Take a last look around, little lady. This place's gonna be abandoned property, this time tomorra'. Free fer the takin'. It's

75

gonna look real differ'nt, real soon. Headquarters, that's what it's gonna be. GHQ fer White America. Ever'thing we need's right out thar in that van. Jest—. (*A clatter from the stair, and in comes an armed Klansman, roughly holding a captive Catherine from behind.*)

BETTY. Catherine!

CATHERINE. I'm sorry—.

OWEN. Hey, purty. 'Uz you hidin' on us, up thar?

CATHERINE. Charlie—.

OWEN. Whar's yer kid brother at?

CATHERINE. He's—. (*To Charlie.*) They got him, Charlie. They got both of us. It was so dark. Ellard—they're tyin' Ellard up, I think. (*Sobbing.*) I'm sorry! Oh, I'm so sorry!

BETTY. Don't blame yerself, honey. You tried. We all of us tried. (*Three Klansmen return from upstairs.*)

OWEN. All right, then. Come on, monkey-boy. Get up on 'at table. Le's see us some monkey-dancin'. Then, maybe we'll think up sump'm else we kin do. Come on, now.

BETTY. Charlie. You better do what he says.

CHARLIE. (*Slowly, with growing power, his eyes boring straight into Owen.*) You—dare—to—affront—me? I, who have lain in wait, lo, these many centuries for such a night as this!

OWEN. What!

CHARLIE. (*Slowly stepping onto the sofa.*) I, child of Hrothgar and of Moloch! I, whom the Old Ones have given suck, to rise now from the forest mold and smite thee! Klatu! Barada! Nikto!

OWEN. Now, don't you start that! I warn ye!

CHARLIE. There are a thousand serpents in my bowels, and each one squeals with pleasure!

OWEN. Now, don't you—don't you start that Hoodoo talk, mister, er somebody's gonna get *hurt.*

CHARLIE. (*In his full glory now, standing majestically atop the sofa.*) You dare to sneer at me! You—puny—earthling!

OWEN. (*Troubled by this unexpected word.*) "Earthling"! What—?

CHARLIE. *Aroint thee, sniveling spawn!* (*The Klansman holding Catherine releases her and raises his rifle. Charlie wheels on him, pointing at him with ramrod-straight arm and outstretched fingers.*) From my heart, I strike at thee! (*With a vengeful cry, Charlie makes a sudden upward slash through the air with his arm, and the Klansman's rifle, as though wrenched from him by an unseen force, flies from his grasp and spins across the floor.*)

KLANSMAN. Wha—?

OWEN. What th'—? (*In a flash, Charlie has returned his arm, so that it points again at the offending Klansman.*) LQ 49 melting — la la. visual

BETTY. Charlie! No! No! (*But there is no stopping Charlie in his wrath. From somewhere deep within him comes a constant, shrill, unearthly sound. We half expect to see glass objects shattering here and there; but instead—can we believe our eyes?—the Klansman claws the air, giving out a cry born of great, searing pain—deep at first, then higher, like the voice of a dwarf, then like that of an insect, as—he grows smaller! His arms retract, his head sinks into his body, and his body itself, writhing in place and possibly seething smoke, slowly melts into the floor, leaving at last only a pile of white and rumpled cloth.*) LQ 51 El head down

OWEN. (*Pause. Staring at the spot.*) Holy shit.

CHARLIE. (*Turning with eyes ablaze to Owen now, and bringing his deadly arm into firing position.*) De bees come down! De bees come down! Gonna look into your *bones*, when de *bees*—*come*—! (*Suddenly conscious of his mortality, Owen flees, crying as he goes the only exit-line really worthy of him.*)

OWEN. *AAAAAAAAAAAAAAAAAAAAAH!*

THE OTHER KLANSMEN. (*Who know a catch-phrase when they hear one.*) *AAAAAAAAAAAAAAAAAAAAAAAH!* (*Betty, Charlie and Catherine watch the scrambling exodus until everyone is gone and the door has slammed. Then they all three rush to the pile of white clothing.*)

CHARLIE. (*Lifting the hood from the pile.*) Are you all right? (*Perhaps we have already guessed.*)

ELLARD. (*Coming up out of the floor—the trap from Scene 2.*) I'm fine.

CATHERINE. You did good, bro!

ELLARD. I know it. (*During the following, Ellard steps out of the trap, reaches in and pulls the trapdoor shut. If a smoke effect has been used, some business might be made of first dousing something down below from an onstage bucket of water.*)

BETTY. You 'uz *all* real good. That even give *me* the shivers.

CATHERINE. My God, Charlie, it worked. It worked!

BETTY. Any more a' those fellas upstairs?

ELLARD. Just that one we conked on the head. Took these off him 'n' he was still asleep.

BETTY. Is he hurt bad?

ELLARD. I don't know, it was too dark.

BETTY. Well, let's get to him before he—. (*They head for the stairs, but stop, seeing the doorway filled with the staggering, shoeless*

77

form of David. He is holding a hand over his bruised, throbbing forehead.)

CATHERINE. David!

DAVID. Where are they?

CATHERINE. David, what in the world—?

DAVID. Where'd they go? What's happened?

ELLARD. Who, the Klan? We scared 'em all off.

DAVID. You—? (*Madly.*) You *can't* have!

ELLARD. We did. It wudn't that hard.

DAVID. You—! That's it, then. That's the end!

CATHERINE. David?

DAVID. Aaah—I was so close! I—it was in my hands, Catherine. It was all—all about to happen!

CATHERINE. What?

DAVID. We just needed the money—.

CATHERINE. The money? What are you talking about?

DAVID. A new nation, Catherine! A Christian, white nation. With these hands, I was bringing it about! With these hands! You and I, Catherine. You and I were going to be right at the forefront of the most powerful Christian force on earth!

CATHERINE. The *Klan*?

DAVID. Yes! The Klan! Yes! The Invisible Empire! Don't you look at me like that! It's true! We could have made this country clean again! Wiped this nation clean of—(*Looking at Charlie.*) people like him!

CATHERINE. David!

DAVID. Foreigners! Jews! Catholics!

CATHERINE. Stop! *Stop* it! What are you talking about? Nobody is like him! Nobody is like anybody!

DAVID. Oh, open your eyes! They're taking it—.

CATHERINE. The money!

DAVID. What?

CATHERINE. Money. You said, "the money"!

DAVID. Catherine—.

CATHERINE. My money. That's why you wanted to marry me!

DAVID. No—.

CATHERINE. You were going to finance the Klan with my money!

DAVID. I loved you, Catherine!

CATHERINE. Then why didn't you tell me? Why didn't you

tell me about this *thing* you were doing?
DAVID. I—.
CATHERINE. *Why!*
DAVID. (*Stamping his foot.*) *I wanted it to be a surprise!* (*Pause.*)
CATHERINE. Get out of here, David. (*David starts backing toward the doorway as he speaks, not seeing Froggy, who has come in the front door, his face hidden by a shockproof helmet. In his gloved hands is his detonator, attached to two wires which trail behind him out the door.*)
DAVID. (*To Catherine.*) All right. But I just want you to remember this day when some foreigner is taking the bread out of—.
FROGGY. (*To David.*) Excuse me.
DAVID. What?
FROGGY. Is that your van outside?
DAVID. My—? The van! They've left me my van! (*Froggy, having heard enough, puts the detonator on the counter and begins arming it.*) Praise God! I can do it alone! I can start again from scratch as long as I've got that—! (*Froggy pushes the plunger down. From outside, there is the sound and flash of a huge explosion. Perhaps a VW hubcap flies through the door.*) The—! The *van!* It blew *up!* *Why?*
FROGGY. (*Taking off his helmet.*) Bloody foreign cars. Yer can't trust 'em, can yer?
DAVID. (*Leaving us, as he departs, with a quote from Owen Musser.*) *AAAAAAAAAAAAAH!*
THE OTHERS. Frog!
FROGGY. Everyone 'ere all right?
CHARLIE. Yes.
FROGGY. (*Glancing after David.*) So—'e was one of 'em too, eh?
BETTY. Yes. He had us all fooled.
CATHERINE. (*Looking at the Klan robes.*) Oh, David. . . .
FROGGY. The cops'll 'ave 'im by now, I expect, Miss. They're down there pickin' up the others by the truckload. Sorry we're late.
CATHERINE. Oh, David. . . .
CHARLIE. (*Gently, as he touches the white robe in Catherine's hand.*) David—? Sheet? Head?
CATHERINE. (*Still watching after him.*) Sheet-head, that's right.
CHARLIE. I am sorry.
CATHERINE. Don't be sorry. Be sorry when I marry a

stranger. Don't be sorry when I don't.

BETTY. (*At the window.*) Frog—you exploded that van?

FROGGY. Yes, love. Sorry about the geraniums.

BETTY. That's all right.

FROGGY. 'Ere, wot 'appened then? 'Ow'd yer get rid of all those blokes?

BETTY. We scairt 'em off! It was Charlie's idea, 'n' then we all acted it out. First Catherine 'n' Ellard went upstairs, 'n' then they hit David over the head with a croquet mallet, jest like that King Buddy used t' do—'n' then they come down again 'n' Charlie kinda went "Wooo!" an' Ellard scooched all down into the floor. (*Pause.*)

FROGGY. Oh.

BETTY. It 'uz *real* scary.

FROGGY. It would be, yeh.

BETTY. So—one thing 'n' another, this has been a real unusual day, fer here. (*Seeing Catherine.*) 'Scuse me, Frog. (*To Catherine.*) Honey, now, don't you grieve.

CATHERINE. (*Turning to her.*) I'm not grievin', Betty. I'm just havin' thoughts about this and that. Listen, I just watched you defendin' this place. You're not gonna move out of this house.

BETTY. I ain't?

CATHERINE. No. 'Cause I'm gonna stay here with you.

BETTY. You are?

CATHERINE. Yep. We're gonna get this place goin' again, you and me. And Ellard, too, if he wants to. How about that, El? Maybe you could do that brickwork.

ELLARD. Sure! An' I was just thinkin' today about how this place could really use like a brick porch, out there, a·'' maybe some little brick walls around all the trees?

CATHERINE. All right, we'll stay then.

BETTY. Good. That'll be the next best thing t' havin' kids. I always did want t' see kids runnin' around here.

CATHERINE. Well, you just keep your eyes open.

BETTY. What?

CATHERINE. Tell you sump'm later.

ELLARD. And maybe some brick—birds?

CATHERINE. Brick birds?

ELLARD. Yeah?

CATHERINE. What *kind* of birds.

ELLARD. Great big?

CATHERINE. Great big brick birds?

ELLARD. Yeah.

CATHERINE. Well, *El*lard?

BETTY. No, now, if Ellard thinks that'd be nice, I'd be inclined to believe him.

CATHERINE. (*Satisfied.*) Well. All right.

ELLARD. 'Kay.

CATHERINE. Charlie, I hate to think what would've happened to us if you hadn't been here. I'm gonna miss you no end.

BETTY. We all will.

ELLARD. (*Sadly.*) Yeah. . . .

CHARLIE. I meess you, too. (*The four of them gather for a big old communal hug.*) Oh. . . . Gol-lee.

CATHERINE. Yeah. . . .

FROGGY. Charlie—. (*The others look at Froggy.*) Could I 'ave a word wiv you, please? (*To the others.*) Sorry. This'll only take a minute. Eh—.

BETTY. That's all right. (*To Ellard and Catherine.*) Y'all come out here with me.

FROGGY. One minute, that's all. (*Catherine, Betty and Ellard leave. When they are alone.*) Look, Charlie—I don't know 'ow to say this, quite. And I didn't think now would be the time for it—but p'raps it is, after all. (*Taking out a telegram and handing it to Charlie.*) This came for you today. (*Charlie reads. As the telegram's contents register, a look of sadness and loss comes over his face.*) So yer see—the point is, if yer'd like ter stay 'ere a few days—or more—it won't make much difference, now, will it? (*Pause.*)

CHARLIE. Ohh. . . . (*Softly, to himself.*) Straznia bolyeeshnyaya, Mavra. Ta lu, Mavra. Ta lu. . . .

FROGGY. Charlie—are you all right?

CHARLIE. (*Still in dialect.*) Yes. All right. Yes.

FROGGY. Charlie—*talk* ter me.

CHARLIE. (*Sweetly, reassuringly, but still in dialect.*) I talk. One-two-three. Hello.

FROGGY. (*Worried.*) Charlie—.

CATHERINE. (*Coming from the kitchen.*) 'Scuse me, I just need to get a—. (*She is stopped by Charlie's downcast look.*) Charlie? What is it? (*The others are entering now and stand by the door.*)

FROGGY. 'E's 'ad some bad news, I'm afraid. (*Points to the telegram.*) Came this mornin'.

CATHERINE. What is it, Charlie? Can you tell me? (*No

81

answer.) Can you whisper it to me? (*Charlie nods, whispers.*) In English, Charlie. (*He whispers again.*) Ohhh, Charlie. (*Hugging Charlie.*) We've both had our losses today, haven't we? (*Charlie nods.*)

FROGGY. I've told 'im 'e could stay 'ere a bit longer, if 'e'd like. I could fix it on my end.

CATHERINE. How about that, Charlie? You want to stay here with us? (*No answer.*) Charlie?

FROGGY. Charlie? Look — I ought ter tell yer — I'm a bit worried about 'im. I ought ter tell yer — 'e's not wot 'e seems. I mean —.

CATHERINE. Shh, now. I think I know.

FROGGY. Yer do? (*She nods.*)

CATHERINE. (*To Charlie.*) Come on, baby. We'll take care of you.

CHARLIE. I — stay?

CATHERINE. (*Leading him to the doorway.*) That's right. You stay. And you know what? I bet, if we work real hard, someday you won't be talkin' with any accent at all, any more.

CHARLIE. That may take long. . . .

CATHERINE. Well. We've got all the time in the world. (*And they are out. Ellard follows.*)

FROGGY. Bet? I'm 'avin' a drink. (*He goes to the bar, pours.*) And I never drink alone. My treat (*He hands her a drink.*) 'Ere you go.

BETTY. My land. What — what was in that telegram he had?

FROGGY. It was from the 'ospital. It was 'is wife.

BETTY. His wife? Did she —? Did she die?

FROGGY. *No.* No. It was *from* 'is wife. No. She recovered completely. Ran off with a proctologist.

BETTY. (*Shakes her head.*) Well — real life's awful hard, sometimes.

FROGGY. It is, Bet. It is that. (*Toasting.*) Blasny, blasny.

BETTY. Blasny, blasny. (*They drink as the lights fade out.*)

THE END

82

PROPERTY PLOT
(Off-Broadway production)

On Stage
Magazines
Pillow
Wall telephone
Map of Georgia
Croquet mallet
2 candlesticks and candles
Volume of Shakespeare
Woodbin with wood and two apples, 1 bite out of each
Coffee table containing:
    Bowl with 3 apples
    Old issue of *People* magazine (Princess Di on cover)
    Assorted games
Hutch containing:
    Display of silver spoons
    Hourglass
    Dish with pens and pencils
    3 bottles of Coke, 1 real
    4 liquor bottles, 1 filled with fresh tea
    8 shot-glasses
    4 tumblers
    1 fresh bottle of seltzer
    3 bottle-openers
    Oil lamp
    2 candlesticks, candles
    Ashtray
    Drawer containing box of candles, napkins
2 wastebins filled with "rubbish"
Corkboard on wall with thumbtacks, notices, room keys labelled 1-7
Sign-in desk containing:
    Register
    Tray with mail
    Bell
    Ashtray
    Box with pens, pencils, pads, souvenir magazines
    Room keys

Offstage
"Kitchen" area, Act I
  Teapot with tea
  Cup and saucer with tea
  Carrot
  Candlestick with candle
  Matches or lighter
  Bowl with biscuit
  Tray with 2 plastic juice glasses, ½ full of orange juice
  Dish of grits, spoon in dish
  Tray with 2 dishes with fried eggs
  2 sets of silverware (fork, spoon, knife)
  2 napkin-holders with napkins
  Salt and pepper shakers
"Kitchen" area, Act II: Tray with
  2 dishes with fried chicken and biscuits
  2 sets silverware in napkins
  2 cups, saucers, ½ full of tea
Elsewhere offstage:
Wheelbarrow containing:
  Bush
  Brick
  Rock
  Leaf
  Nail
  Mason jar
  Board
Harmonica
Hubcap
Canvas wood-carrier, 2 logs (Betty)
Assorted mail (Catherine)
Newspaper (Atlanta *Constitution*)
Bullhorn (Owen)
Baseball bat ⎫
Flashlights ⎬ (Klansmen)
Shotgun   ⎪
Bullwhip   ⎭
Rubber hose (Owen)
"Condemned" certificate (Owen)
Telegram (Froggy)

84

Box, tied with string, containing:
  Bundle of dynamite
  Assorted papers
  Crumpled newspaper
  Crumpled newspaper
Hourglass
Suitcase (Charlie)
Detonator (Froggy)
3 spoons tied in fabric case (Froggy)
Switchblade knife (Owen)
Map of Georgia (Froggy)
Sauerkraut (under trap)
Mason jar (under trap)
Walkie-talkie

PRODUCTION NOTES

In both the Milwaukee and the Off-Broadway productions of *The Foreigner*, the trickiest thing to nail down in rehearsal has been the nature of the characters and their relationships at the beginning of the play, i.e. before Charlie changes things around. One point, of course, is to lead the audience to make certain character-judgments which later prove wrong; so it's important that they at first perceive David as genuinely decent; Catherine as shrill, spoiled, and spiteful; and Ellard as hopelessly backward. Charlie, too, must seem genuinely, if sweetly, dull. Also, for the sake of plot dynamics, it's vital to show our protagonists losing and at each other's throats, and our villains confident and on the verge of victory as the tale begins. The unhappier Betty, Catherine, and Ellard are with one another and themselves at the outset, the more successful the reversal can be.

Speaking of villains, let there be no such thing as "comedy villains" here. Our malefactors must be, within the style of the play, the real thing — obsessive, cunning, and dangerous. They will be funny, but only if they can first make us recoil.

A note about Charlie's "language". The two Charlies I've worked with, Al Brooks and Tony Heald, both discovered that inventing Charlie's "language" pays off best if it seems a tentative, difficult process, rather than a glib, sudden talent. As played, both only gained complete confidence in their abilities somewhere in the middle of the long nonsense-story.

Larry Shue

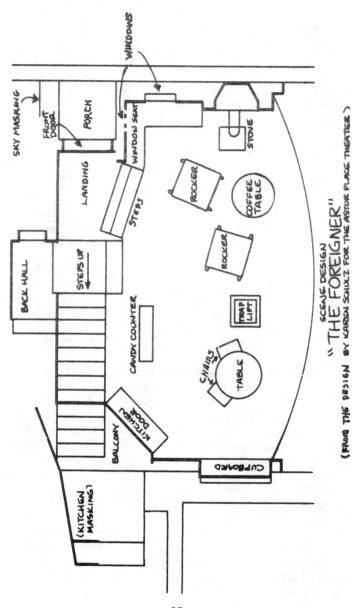

SCENE DESIGN
"THE FOREIGNER"

(FROM THE DESIGN BY KAREN SCHULZ FOR THE ASTOR PLACE THEATER)

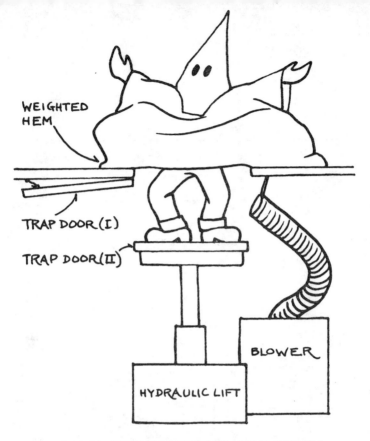

WEIGHTED HEM

TRAP DOOR (I)

TRAP DOOR (II)

BLOWER

HYDRAULIC LIFT

NOTE ON SPECIAL EFFECT IN ACT II, SCENE 2
(Ellard's disappearance)

In Milwaukee and New York, Ellard's disappearance during the Klan's visit was achieved with the help of a hydraulic lift beneath the trap, which would lower slowly on cue. In Milwaukee, the hinged trap door used in I. 2. was replaced at intermission with an identical "door" — actually the top of the lift platform. Probably, by using a counter-weighted platform, the descent could be achieved manually, as well. On Ellard's Klan costume, the circumference of the hem should be stiffened and weighted, so that it encircles the trap as Ellard sinks. The last key element is wind blowing upward through the trap; this fills out the costume as Ellard sinks, preventing the costume from following him into the trap. Recorded weather or ethereal noises can be used to cover the sound of the necessary machinery. In New York, smoke and lights were also used beneath the trap, to good effect.